Ready-to-Use
VOCABULARY, WORD ANALYSIS & COMPREHENSION ACTIVITIES

Third Grade Reading Level

HENRIETTE L. ALLEN, Ph.D.
WALTER B. BARBE, Ph.D.

D1507459

THE CENTER FOR APPLIED
RESEARCH IN EDUCATION
West Nyack, New York 10994

Library of Congress Cataloging-in-Publication Data

Allen, Henriette L.
    Ready-to-use vocabulary, word analysis & comprehension activities
/ Henriette L. Allen, Walter B. Barbe, Linda Lehner.
        p.   cm. — (Reading skills activities library)
    Contents: [1] First grade reading level — [2] Second grade
reading level — [3] Third grade reading level.
    ISBN 0-87628-932-4 (v. 1). — ISBN 0-87628-933-2 (v. 2).—ISBN
0-87628-934-0 (v. 3)
    1. Reading (Elementary)—Problems, exercises, etc.   2. Reading
comprehension—Problems, exercises, etc.   3. Vocabulary—Study and
teaching (Elementary)—Problems, exercises, etc.   I. Barbe, Walter
Burke, 1926– . II. Lehner, Linda.   III. Title.   IV. Series.
LB1573.A44   1996
372.4—dc20   96-18332
                                                                    CIP

© 1996 *by* The Center for Applied Research in Education, West Nyack, NY

Printed in the United States of America

10 9 8 7 6 5 4 3

ISBN 0-87628-934-0

**THE CENTER FOR APPLIED RESEARCH
IN EDUCATION**

©1996 by Prentice-Hall, Inc.

On the World Wide Web at http://www.phdirect.com

About the READING SKILLS ACTIVITIES LIBRARY

The "Reading Skills Activities Library" is designed to give classroom teachers, reading specialists, and others who teach reading multiple learning activities to build specific reading skills at each grade level, first through third grade. Each grade level unit provides 200 or more reproducible reading and writing activities to help children master reading skills that can be used with *any* reading program.

FIRST LEVEL *Ready-to-Use Vocabulary, Word Analysis & Comprehension Activities*—**FIRST GRADE READING LEVEL**

SECOND LEVEL *Ready-to-Use Vocabulary, Word Analysis & Comprehension Activities*—**SECOND GRADE READING LEVEL**

THIRD LEVEL *Ready-to-Use Vocabulary, Word Analysis & Comprehension Activities*—**THIRD GRADE READING LEVEL**

The skill activities follow the sequence in the Reading Skills Check Lists developed by nationally known educator Walter B. Barbe, Ph.D. The activities can be assigned to individuals or groups and supervised by the teacher, a paraprofessional, a parent, a volunteer, or a peer.

Each grade level unit of Reading Skills Activities includes:

1. Directions for using the reading activities at that level to support direct instruction
2. At least 200 reproducible activities for quick, reliable practice or enrichment of each reading skill, with answer keys at the end
3. A reproducible Reading Skills Check List for the major skill areas covered at that level for easy individual or group recordkeeping

You will find that the "Reading Skills Activities Library" provides for:

- Quick, accurate prescriptive help to meet specific reading needs
- A minimum of four ready-to-use reading skills exercises to reinforce, supplement, and enrich instruction in each skill
- Flexibility in planning individual and group activities, homework assignments, and peer- or aide-assisted instruction

The activities can be used by the teacher, parent or reading specialist in any learning setting, in any manner the teacher deems most appropriate. The activities are meant to provide handy, efficient, systematic help in developing reading skills that students need to become proficient readers.

Henriette L. Allen
Walter B. Barbe

About the Authors

Henriette L. Allen, Ph.D.

Henriette L. Allen, Ph.D., is a former classroom teacher in the schools of Coventry, Rhode Island, the Aramco Schools of Dhahran, Saudi Arabia, The American Community School of Benghazi, Libya, and Jackson, Mississippi. Dr. Allen served in several administrative roles, including assistant superintendent of the Jackson Public Schools. She is presently an education consultant recognized nationally. Dr. Allen is the senior author of the series *Competency Tests for Basic Reading Skills* (West Nyack, NY: The Center for Applied Research in Education.) She has taught reading skills at both elementary and secondary levels, has supervised the development of a Continuous Progress Reading Program for the Jackson Public Schools, and has lectured widely in the fields of reading, classroom management, technology in the classroom, and leadership in educational administration. Dr. Allen is listed in the *World Who's Who of Women* and *Who's Who—School District Officials*. She was the 1996 recipient of the Distinguished Service Award given by the American Association of School Administrators.

Walter B. Barbe, Ph.D.

A nationally known authority in the fields of reading and learning disabilities, Walter B. Barbe, Ph.D., was for twenty-five years editor-in-chief of the widely acclaimed magazine *Highlights for Children*, and adjunct professor at The Ohio State University. Dr. Barbe is the author of over 150 professional articles and a number of books, including *Personalized Reading Instruction* (West Nyack, NY: Parker Publishing Company, Inc.), coauthored with Jerry L. Abbot. He is also the senior author and editor of two series—*Creative Growth with Handwriting* (Columbus, OH: Zaner-Bloser, Inc.) and *Barbe Reading Skills Check Lists and Activities* (West Nyack, NY: The Center for Applied Research in Education, Inc.)—and he is senior editor of *Competency Tests for Basic Reading Skills*. Dr. Barbe is a fellow of the American Psychological Association and is listed in *Who's Who in America* and *American Men of Science*.

Contents

About the Reading Skills Activities Library **3**

How to Use These Reading Skills Activities Most Effectively **9**

    Identifying Individual Reading Needs • 9
    Teaching and Reinforcing Skills • 10
    Recordkeeping on the Skills Check List • 10

Reading Skills Check List — THIRD LEVEL **11**

Vocabulary, Word Analysis & Comprehension Activities —
    THIRD LEVEL **15**

• **VOCABULARY**

    A. Recognizes Dolch 220 Basic Sight Words • 18–23

    B. Word Meaning:
       1. Comprehends and Uses Correctly the Following Words: • 24
          a. Function words • 24–28
          b. Direction words • 29–31
          c. Action words • 32–35
          d. Forms of address • 36–38
          e. Career words • 39–42
          f. Color words • 43–45
          g. Metric words • 46–48
          h. Curriculum words • 49–53

• **WORD ANALYSIS**

    A. Refines Phonics Skills:
       1. Initial consonant sounds • 54–59
       2. Short and long vowel sounds • 60–64
       3. Changes in words by:
          a. adding *s, es, d, ed, ing, er, est* • 65–67
          b. dropping final *e* and adding *ing* • 68–69
            a.–b. Review • 70–74
          c. doubling the consonant before adding *ing* • 75–79
          d. changing *y* to *i* before adding *es* • 80–84
            a.–d. Review • 85–89
       4. Vowel rules:
          a. vowel in one-syllable word is short • 90–91
          b. vowel in syllable or word ending in *e* is long • 92–93
            a.–b. Review • 94

Contents

   c.   two vowels together, first is often long and second is silent • 95–97
   d.   vowel alone in word is short • 98–99
      a.–d. Review • 100–104
5.   *C* followed by *i, e, y* makes *s* sound • 105–109
      C followed by *a, o, u* makes *k* sound
6.   *G* followed by *i, e, y* makes *j* sound • 110–114
      G followed by *a, o, u* makes *guh* sound
7.   Silent letters in *kn, wr, gn* • 115–119

B. Knows Skills of:
1.   Forming plurals • 120–124
      by adding *s, es, ies*
      by changing *f* to *v* and adding *es*
2.   Similarities of sound such as *x* and *cks* (box—blocks) • 125–129
3.   Roman numerals I through X • 130–134

C. Knows Syllabication Rules
1.   There are usually as many syllables in a word as there are vowels • 135–129
2.   When there is a single consonant between two vowels, and the first vowel is long, the consonant belongs in the second syllable (pu/pil). When the first vowel is short, the consonant belongs in the first syllable (sec/ond) • 140–144
3.   When there is a double consonant, the syllable break is between the two consonants and one is silent (lit/tle) • 145–149

D. Can Hyphenate Words Using Syllable Rules • 150–154

E. Understands Use of Primary Accent Mark • 155–159

F. Knows to Accent First Syllable, Unless it is a Prefix, Otherwise Accent Second Syllable • 160–164

• **COMPREHENSION**

A. Can Find Main Idea in Story • 165–169

B. Can Keep Events in Proper Sequence • 170–175

C. Can Draw Logical Conclusions • 176–180

D. Can See Relationships • 181–185

E. Can Predict Outcomes • 186–190

F. Can Follow Printed Directions • 191–195

G. Can Read for a Definite Purpose • 196–205
    1. For pleasure
    2. To obtain answer to question
    3. To obtain general idea of content

H. Can Classify Items • 206–210

 I. Can Use Index • 211–215

J. Can Alphabetize Words by First Two Letters • 216–220

K. Knows Technique of Skimming • 221–225

L. Can Determine Source to Obtain Information • 226–230

M. Can Use Maps and Charts • 231–235

Answer Key **235**

    VOCABULARY • 235–237

    WORD ANALYSIS • 237–246

    COMPREHENSION • 247–251

Class Record of Reading Skills: THIRD LEVEL • 253

How to Use These Reading Skills Activities Most Effectively

The learning activities in this unit can help you make optimal use of time in helping each of your students learn to read. The first requirement for a positive learning situation is, of course, your own enthusiastic teaching. Nothing replaces that. However, the student must apply what has been taught. Instruction must be followed through. Practice is needed in order to be sure that a skill has not only been learned but mastered.

In order for skills to develop sequentially, it is vital that you know where a student is within the sequence of reading skills. The Reading Skills Check List and practice activities in this unit provide a practical and systematic means to meet the specific reading skill needs of each of your pupils on a continuing, day-to-day basis.

The reading activities offer ready-to-use opportunities to learn, practice, and master the vocabulary, word analysis, and comprehension skills at the third grade level, including at least four pages of practice work directed to each skill. Each activity is tailored to meet the learning needs of students at the third grade level. The activities provide complete, easy-to-follow student directions and may be duplicated as many times as needed for individual or group use. Complete answer keys are provided at the end of the unit.

The Reading Skills Check List is *not* intended as a rigid instructional program. Rather, it is meant to offer a general pattern around which a program may be built. The check list may be used to verify (1) where the student is in a sequence of reading skills, (2) when the student masters the skills, and (3) the number of skills mastered.

A copy of the Reading Skills Check List: THIRD LEVEL is on pages 14–16 for your optional use.

IDENTIFYING INDIVIDUAL READING NEEDS

Before planning an instructional program for any pupil, it is necessary to determine at what level the student is reading. This may be accomplished through the use of an informal reading inventory. Many such informal assessment devices are provided in *Alternative Assessment Techniques for Reading & Writing* (West Nyack, NY: The Center for Applied Research in Education, 1996), by Wilma H. Miller.

Once a pupil's areas of difficulty are identified, instruction can then be planned, taught, and reinforced through practice. When the student has worked through a unit of instruction, a posttest to verify mastery of the skill may be given. When mastery occurs, the student progresses to another skill. When the student is unsuccessful in a specific reading skill and a reasonable amount of instruction does not result in mastery, it may be that a different instructional method or approach is needed, or a preliminary skill needs reevaluation followed by additional teaching-learning activities.

TEACHING AND REINFORCING SKILLS

After a reading skill has been identified as lacking, the teaching-learning process begins. The skill may be taught using the basal reader, selected children's literature, and/or your reading program as the basic source of information. Explaining the skill, giving the rules which apply, and illustrating by examples are frequently used techniques. The next step in the teaching-learning process is to assign an activity with which the student can try his or her wings at learning. The activity indicates if the learning has occurred or verifies that the student understands the lesson. When the student meets that particular situation in a reading selection, he or she can apply the appropriate reading skill.

At this point in the learning process, the reading skills activities should become a valuable teaching asset. They include several pages of practice exercises for every reading objective on the reading skills check list as well as those found in every reading program. You can select the exercises specifically designed to aid students at their particular level of reading development. After the paper-and-pencil activities are completed—during class time, as a homework assignment, as a cooperative learning activity, or as a peer instruction activity—results of the learning activity should be discussed with the student. You can then prescribe additional practice for the skill, reteach the skill, or proceed to the next activity.

RECORDKEEPING ON THE SKILLS CHECK LIST

Recordkeeping is an important part of any instructional design. Simplicity and ease are vital. One suggested method for marking the skills check list is as follows.

B. Structural Analysis
   1. Knows endings
      a. *ed* sound as "ed" in *wanted*
      b. *ed* sound as "d" in *moved*
      c. *ed* sound as "t" in *liked*
   2. Recognizes compound words
      (*into, upon*)
   3. Knows common word families

M		
8/20	M	9/28
M		

all ___	an ___	ell ___	ook ___	in
at ___	ill ___	ay ___	ing ___	ish
it ___	et ___	ake ___	ack ___	ight

C. Word Form Clues
   1. Recognizes upper- and lower-case letters

Put an *M* in the first column if the pupil takes a test and demonstrates mastery of that basic reading skill. If the pupil has not mastered the skill, record the date. The date in the first column then indicates when instruction in the skill began. When the pupil is tested a second time, put an *M* in the second column if mastery is achieved and record the date of mastery in the next column. Thus, anyone looking at the check list can tell whether the student mastered the skill before instruction or after instruction began, and when the skill was actually mastered.

Reading Skills Check List
THIRD LEVEL

On the following pages you will find the Reading Skills Check List: THIRD LEVEL. A group or individual recordkeeping form, "Class Record of Reading Skills: THIRD LEVEL," is also provided on pages 253–255.

Together, these forms offer a practical and optional individual and group record-keeping system for pinpointing students' reading progress throughout the school year. They provide a useful guide to instruction as well as a basis for conferences with other faculty, parents, and the student about the pupil's reading progress. These records can also be passed along to the next grade level teacher at the end of the year to provide evidence of where students are in the continuum of reading skills.

READING SKILLS CHECK LIST
THIRD LEVEL*

_____

(Last Name)   (First Name)   (Name of School)

(Age)   (Grade Placement)   (Name of Teacher)

I. Vocabulary:

   A.   Recognizes Dolch 220 Basic Sight Words

___ a	___ don't	___ if	___ over	___ they
___ about	___ down	___ in	___ own	___ think
___ after	___ draw	___ into	___ pick	___ this
___ again	___ drink	___ is	___ play	___ those
___ all	___ eat	___ it	___ please	___ three
___ always	___ eight	___ its	___ pretty	___ to
___ am	___ every	___ jump	___ pull	___ today
___ an	___ fall	___ just	___ put	___ together
___ and	___ far	___ keep	___ ran	___ too
___ any	___ fast	___ kind	___ read	___ try
___ are	___ find	___ know	___ red	___ two
___ around	___ first	___ laugh	___ ride	___ under
___ ask	___ five	___ let	___ right	___ up
___ at	___ fly	___ light	___ round	___ upon
___ ate	___ for	___ like	___ run	___ us
___ away	___ found	___ little	___ said	___ use
___ be	___ four	___ live	___ saw	___ very
___ because	___ from	___ long	___ say	___ walk
___ been	___ full	___ look	___ see	___ want
___ before	___ funny	___ made	___ seven	___ warm
___ best	___ gave	___ make	___ shall	___ was
___ better	___ get	___ many	___ she	___ wash
___ big	___ give	___ may	___ show	___ we
___ black	___ go	___ me	___ sing	___ well
___ blue	___ goes	___ much	___ sit	___ went
___ both	___ going	___ must	___ six	___ were
___ bring	___ good	___ my	___ sleep	___ what
___ brown	___ got	___ myself	___ small	___ when
___ but	___ green	___ never	___ so	___ where
___ buy	___ grow	___ new	___ some	___ which
___ by	___ had	___ no	___ soon	___ white
___ call	___ has	___ not	___ start	___ who
___ came	___ have	___ now	___ stop	___ why
___ can	___ he	___ of	___ take	___ will
___ carry	___ help	___ off	___ tell	___ wish
___ clean	___ her	___ old	___ ten	___ with
___ cold	___ here	___ on	___ thank	___ work
___ come	___ him	___ once	___ that	___ would
___ could	___ his	___ one	___ the	___ write
___ cut	___ hold	___ only	___ their	___ yellow
___ did	___ hot	___ open	___ them	___ yes
___ do	___ how	___ or	___ then	___ you
___ does	___ hurt	___ our	___ there	___ your
___ done	___ I	___ out	___ these	

* © 1996 Walter B. Barbe, Honesdale, PA 18431.

B. Word Meaning:
   1. Comprehends and uses correctly the following words.

a. Function Words	**b. Direction Words**	**e. Career Words**	**h. Curriculum Words**
___against	___around	___artist	___add
___also	___backward	___factory	___American
___being	___forward	___lawyer	___country
___during	___left	___mechanic	___ecology
___each	___right	___money	___even
___end	___toward	___nurse	___fall
___enough	**c. Action Words**	___office	___few
___men	___carry	___operator	___greater
___more	___draw	___teacher	___less
___most	___kick	___training	___number
___other	___push	___vocation	___odd
___same	___skate	**f. Color Words**	___seasons
___should	___swim	___brown	___set
___since	___think	___green	___space
___such	___throw	___orange	___spring
___than	___travel	___purple	___state
___though	**d. Forms of Address**	**g. Metric Words**	___subtract
___thought	___Miss	___centigrade	___summer
___through	___Mr.	___gram	___United States
___while	___Mrs.	___liter	___winter
___women	___Ms.	___meter	___world

a.

b.

c.

d.

e.

f.

g.

h.

II. Word Analysis:
   A. Refines Phonics Skills:
      1. Initial consonant sounds
      2. Short and long vowel sounds
      3. Changes in words by:
         a. adding *s, es, d, ed, ing, er, est*
         b. dropping final *e* and adding *ing*
         c. doubling the consonant before adding *ing*
         d. changing *y* to *i* before adding *es*
      4. Vowel rules
         a. vowel in one-syllable word is short
         b. vowel in syllable or word ending in *e* is long
         c. two vowels together, first is often long and second is silent
         d. vowel alone in word is short
      5. *C* followed by *i, e, y* makes *s* sound
         C followed by *a, o, u* makes *k* sound
      6. *G* followed by *i, e, y* makes *j* sound
         G followed by *a, o, u* makes *guh* sound
      7. Silent letters in *kn, wr, gn*
   B. Knows Skills of:
      1. Forming plurals
      2. Similarities of sound
      3. Roman numerals I through X
   C. Knows Syllabication Rules
      1. There are usually as many syllables in a word as there are vowels
      2. When there is a single consonant between two vowels, and the first vowel is long, the consonant belongs in the second syllable (pu/pil). When the first vowel is short, the consonant belongs in the first syllable (sec/ond)
      3. When there is a double consonant, the syllable break is between the two consonants and one is silent (lit/tle)
   D. Can Hyphenate Words Using Syllable Rules
   E. Understands Use of Primary Accent Mark
   F. Knows to Accent First Syllable Unless It Is a Prefix

III. Comprehension:

A. Can Find Main Idea in Story
B. Can Keep Events in Proper Sequence
C. Can Draw Logical Conclusions
D. Can See Relationships
E. Can Predict Outcomes
F. Can Follow Printed Directions
G. Can Read for a Definite Purpose
H. Can Classify Items
I. Can Use Index
J. Can Alphabetize Words by First Two Letters
K. Knows Technique of Skimming
L. Can Determine Source to Obtain Information (dictionary, encyclopedia, index, glossary, etc.)
M. Can Use Maps and Charts

Vocabulary, Word Analysis
& Comprehension
Activities
THIRD LEVEL

The following reinforcement activities will help you give students practice in the specific vocabulary, word analysis, and comprehension skills at the THIRD LEVEL. These materials provide for the following:

- Learning activities for specific reading skills
- Individual and group practice and/or enrichment
- Better understanding of classwork
- Verification of skill mastery
- Corrective exercises in specific skills
- Homework activity directed to specific reading needs
- Practice for mastery
- Optimal use of teacher time

The exercises can be photocopied just as they appear for classroom use.
Complete answer keys for activities in this unit are provided on pages 235–251.

DIRECTIONS TO THE TEACHER

For purposes here, the Dolch 220 basic sight words have been divided into five groups to provide several teaching options. You may want to verify the students' knowledge of the words in segments. You may want a student to work with another student on mastery of the words. The word sheets can also be used for individual study and may be sent home to encourage parent assistance in the students' learning.

NOTE: *Check only those words on the sheet that are not recognized.*

Some specific activity suggestions follow:

1. Have a race to see which students recognize the 220 words. Divide the race into five stages. Give the student the option of taking home each sheet he or she masters. Use stars or praising statements for individual achievement.

2. Make 3″ x 4″ cards of each word for classroom study, peer-assisted study, or parent-guided drill.

3. Laminate drill sheets so that they can be used over again.

4. Play a game with 3″ x 4″ cards of the basic sight words. A student collects every card he or she recognizes and plays until a word is missed. The next student then tries. The student with the greatest number of cards is the winner. The goal is to master the entire list of basic sight words.

VOCABULARY   A. Recognizes Dolch 220 Basic Sight Words

Part I

____ a	____ ate	____ buy
____ about	____ away	____ by
____ after	____ be	____ call
____ again	____ because	____ came
____ all	____ been	____ can
____ always	____ before	____ carry
____ am	____ best	____ clean
____ an	____ better	____ cold
____ and	____ big	____ come
____ any	____ black	____ could
____ are	____ blue	____ cut
____ around	____ both	____ did
____ as	____ bring	____ do
____ ask	____ brown	____ does
____ at	____ but	

Part II

_____ done	_____ for	_____ grow
_____ don't	_____ found	_____ had
_____ down	_____ four	_____ has
_____ draw	_____ from	_____ have
_____ drink	_____ full	_____ he
_____ eat	_____ funny	_____ help
_____ eight	_____ gave	_____ her
_____ every	_____ get	_____ here
_____ fall	_____ give	_____ him
_____ far	_____ go	_____ his
_____ fast	_____ goes	_____ hold
_____ find	_____ going	_____ hot
_____ first	_____ good	_____ how
_____ five	_____ got	_____ hurt
_____ fly	_____ green	

VOCABULARY   **A. Recognizes Dolch 220 Basic Sight Words**

Part III

_____ I	_____ like	_____ new
_____ if	_____ little	_____ no
_____ in	_____ live	_____ not
_____ into	_____ long	_____ now
_____ is	_____ look	_____ of
_____ it	_____ made	_____ off
_____ its	_____ make	_____ old
_____ jump	_____ many	_____ on
_____ just	_____ may	_____ once
_____ keep	_____ me	_____ one
_____ kind	_____ much	_____ only
_____ know	_____ must	_____ open
_____ laugh	_____ my	_____ or
_____ let	_____ myself	_____ our
_____ light	_____ never	

VOCABULARY   A. Recognizes Dolch 220 Basic Sight Words

Part IV

_____ out	_____ run	_____ some
_____ over	_____ said	_____ soon
_____ own	_____ saw	_____ start
_____ pick	_____ say	_____ stop
_____ play	_____ see	_____ take
_____ please	_____ seven	_____ tell
_____ pretty	_____ shall	_____ ten
_____ pull	_____ she	_____ thank
_____ put	_____ show	_____ that
_____ ran	_____ sing	_____ the
_____ read	_____ sit	_____ their
_____ red	_____ six	_____ them
_____ ride	_____ sleep	_____ then
_____ right	_____ small	_____ there
_____ round	_____ so	

VOCABULARY   A. Recognizes Dolch 220 Basic Sight Words

Part V

_____ these	_____ us	_____ which
_____ they	_____ use	_____ white
_____ think	_____ very	_____ who
_____ this	_____ walk	_____ why
_____ those	_____ want	_____ will
_____ three	_____ warm	_____ wish
_____ to	_____ was	_____ with
_____ today	_____ wash	_____ work
_____ together	_____ we	_____ would
_____ too	_____ well	_____ write
_____ try	_____ went	_____ yellow
_____ two	_____ were	_____ yes
_____ under	_____ what	_____ you
_____ up	_____ when	_____ your
_____ upon	_____ where	

VOCABULARY   B. Word Meaning   1. a. Function words

DIRECTIONS: Circle the word that best completes the sentence.

1. _____ girl was given a yellow and green T-shirt.
   Same   End   While   Each

2. The ghosts did much damage _____ the night.
   also   during   enough   since

3. _____ of the students were back in school on Monday.
   Most   Same   Than   End

4. Sam asked for _____ ice cream.
   such   more   since   while

5. George's bike is the _____ as Grace's.
   should   since   same   such

6. _____ Annie share her candy?
   Should   Since   Same   Such

7. Suzie has more marbles _____ Ed.
   also   than   through   women

8. Marcus placed his scooter _____ the rail.
   other   while   enough   against

9. The pilot was _____ careful as he landed the plane.
   men   being   should   while

10. At the _____ of the game, the score was 10 to 11.
    enough   end   than   though

11. Dan _____ for a long time before he decided what to do.
    than   though   enough   thought

12. The girls were playing like _____ at a tea party.
    while   end   each   women

VOCABULARY   **B. Word Meaning**   **1. a.** Function words

DIRECTIONS: Circle the word that best completes the sentence.

1. Juan _____ likes popcorn.

         than   also   enough   more

2. When the giraffe had had _____ to eat, he walked to the other end of his pen.

        then   also   enough   most

3. The tunnel was dug by hardworking _____ .

        men   more   most   same

4. Where is the _____ shoe?

        while   thought   since   other

5. _____ 1910, the castle has been deserted.

        Such   Since   While   Most

6. No one had ever seen _____ a monster.

        end   while   than   such

7. The fireman was brave even _____ there was great danger.

        though   while   being   thought

8. The girls baked a cake _____ their mother was napping.

        against   enough   while   through

9. Eight inches of snow fell _____ the night.

        also   other   same   during

10. The jet flew _____ the rainstorm.

        other   through   while   men

11. After eating three pieces of pie, the boys had had _____ .

        same   enough   other   most

12. The children played _____ waiting for the bus.

        while   since   most   also

VOCABULARY   B. Word Meaning   1. a. Function words

DIRECTIONS: Match each word with its correct meaning.

A. ____ 1. each
     ____ 2. against
     ____ 3. during
     ____ 4. end
     ____ 5. through
     ____ 6. same

a. last part
b. just alike
c. from one end to the other
d. every one
e. at some time in
f. directly opposite

B. ____ 1. woman
     ____ 2. since
     ____ 3. should
     ____ 4. man
     ____ 5. thought
     ____ 6. more

a. what a person thinks
b. male person
c. from a past time till now
d. greater in amount
e. female person
f. ought to

VOCABULARY   **B. Word Meaning**   **1. a.** Function words

DIRECTIONS: Choosing from the words above each of the following groups of sentences, write the word that will best fill the blank in each sentence.

also   more   being   other

1. Claire won _____ marbles than Dan.

2. The _____ night, I went to the movies.

3. Suzanne was _____ nice to the elderly woman.

4. She was kind to the blind man _____ .

such   than   through   while

5. The arrow went _____ the cowboy's hat.

6. Gary is taller _____ Marc.

7. _____ you are gone, Mother will sew.

8. It was _____ a bad storm!

though   enough   most   during

9. The boys ate the apples _____ their lunch period.

10. Three inches of rain is _____ rain for one day.

11. Wilfred sold the _____ popcorn.

12. Even _____ Paul was told to drive slowly, he did not listen.

VOCABULARY   B. Word Meaning   1. a. Function words

DIRECTIONS: Choose the word that best completes the sentence and write the word in the blank.

1. The _____ of the story was sad.
   end   each   enough   being

2. The _____ wore jeans.
   such   than   since   men

3. Mother is _____ the children climbing trees.
   since   against   while   woman

4. The giant _____ he had won the race.
   end   during   thought   being

5. Spring comes _____ the month of March.
   during   more   most   than

6. _____ day is a good day.
   Most   Other   Each   While

7. Six men were _____ to move the piano.
   thought   most   more   enough

8. The basket _____ be painted red.
   against   should   end   each

9. The twins wore the _____ kind of shoes.
   same   since   also   men

10. _____ 1950, the Steelers have won all of their games.
    Women   While   Since   Enough

11. The _____ were busy canning the fruit.
    end   other   same   women

12. _____ of the snow fell in the mountains.
    Such   Against   Most   Men

VOCABULARY   B. Word Meaning   1. b. Direction words

DIRECTIONS: Choose the word that best completes the sentence and write the word in the blank.

around   backward   forward   left   right   toward

1. The yellow ribbon was tied _____ the package.

2. The boy blinked his eyes as the ball came _____ him.

3. Inch by inch the worm went _____ up the vine.

4. The opposite of forward is _____ .

5. Most people use their _____ hands to write.

6. A few people use their _____ hands to sew.

7. The bullet zoomed _____ the target.

8. The girls went walking _____ the park.

9. When I put my foot on the gas, the car will move

   _____ .

10. The ball player was not in left field, but he was in

    _____ field.

11. Everyone likes to move forward and not _____ .

12. The leader said to begin marching with our right feet and not

    with our _____ feet.

VOCABULARY   **B. Word Meaning**   **1. b.** Direction words

A. DIRECTIONS: Begin just above point A and draw a line toward ⊞ . Just before you reach ⊞ , draw a circle around ⊞ . Then, continue the line toward B. Go around point B and then go backward toward ☰ by drawing the line under the 00. Just after you pass ☰ , draw a line to the left of the upright line and turn a sharp right at C to D. At D, go upward to X and move forward to Y.

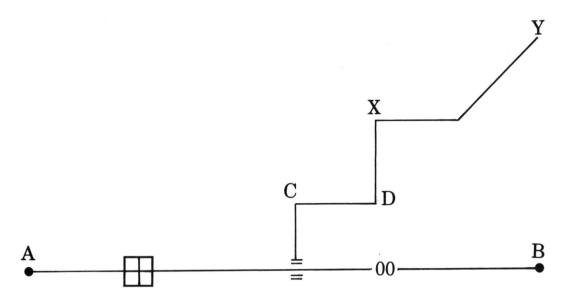

B. DIRECTIONS: Draw a circle around 2. Put your pencil on 1 and draw a line to 4 and then to the left to 3. Go forward to 0. Draw the line backward to 2 and then right to W.

1•   2•   W
                                           •

0
•   •   •
          3   4

VOCABULARY   B. Word Meaning   1. b. Direction words

DIRECTIONS: Choose the word that best completes the sentence and write the word in the blank.

around   backward   forward   left   right   toward

1. The family sat _____ the table eating lunch.

2. In stormy weather, cars move _____ slowly.

3. The swimmer moved quickly _____ the finish line.

4. When you read, you begin on the _____ side of the page.

5. The opposite of left is _____ .

6. To move opposite of forward is to move _____ .

7. She put her sweater on wrong, so it was on _____ .

8. The children sat _____ the fire and sang.

9. The snake moved _____ .

10. You wrote your name on this page in the _____-hand corner.

11. The car came speeding _____ the children.

12. The date on this page is on the _____-hand side of the paper.

VOCABULARY   B. Word Meaning   1. c. Action words

DIRECTIONS: Match each word with its correct meaning.

_____ 1. carry

_____ 2. draw

_____ 3. kick

_____ 4. push

_____ 5. skate

_____ 6. swim

_____ 7. think

_____ 8. throw

_____ 9. travel

a. strike with the foot

b. move along on a blade or wheels

c. use the mind

d. toss an item

e. make a picture

f. go from one place to another

g. take a package from one place to another

h. move along in the water by using arms and legs

i. press hard against something

VOCABULARY   B. Word Meaning   1. c. Action words

DIRECTIONS: In the blank, write the word that best completes the sentence.

carry   draws   kick

1. Tom will _____ the pail to the well.

2. Mules like to _____ .

3. An artist is one who _____ .

push   skate   swim

4. He went to the pool to _____ .

5. To ice _____ is good exercise in the winter.

6. You must _____ on the door to open it.

think   throw   travel

7. You must _____ before you write.

8. Paul likes to _____ the ball to his little sister.

9. A train is a good way to _____ .

kick   push   think

10. The teacher said to _____ the ball along the ground.

11. Do you _____ it will snow?

12. She will _____ the car out of the carport.

VOCABULARY   B. Word Meaning   1. c. Action words

DIRECTIONS: Put an X through the word that best completes the sentence.

1. The wagon can _____ three men.

    draw   kick   carry

2. The plane will _____ at 600 miles an hour.

    push   travel   skate

3. My sister likes to _____ pictures of horses.

    think   draw   swim

4. Don't _____ away the newspapers.

    throw   travel   skate

5. Anger is no reason to _____ anyone.

    draw   kick   think

6. In the summer, Bob likes to _____ in the pond.

    throw   push   swim

7. Please _____ the door closed.

    push   travel   carry

8. To solve the problem, the student must _____.

    carry   draw   think

9. Tony fell down when he tried to _____.

    think   skate   travel

10. Claire will _____ the baby to the doctor's office.

    carry   swim   skate

VOCABULARY   B. Word Meaning   1. c. Action words

DIRECTIONS: Select the word that best completes the sentence. Write the word in the space provided.

travel   throw   think

1. The miner used his mule to _____ to the gold mine.

2. Did she _____ the reins over the horse's head?

3. If you _____ about the problem, you may find several answers.

draw   push   swim

4. Mother taught the baby how to _____ .

5. The man will _____ the wagon up the hill.

6. The artist will _____ your picture for five dollars.

carry   kick   skate

7. Phillip helped to _____ the groceries home.

8. The player did not _____ the ball in time to score.

9. Can you ice _____?

travel   draw   swim

10. How does a duck learn to _____?

11. Tom wants to learn to _____ and to paint.

12. The man liked to _____ by train.

VOCABULARY   **B. Word Meaning**   **1. d.** Forms of address

---

A. DIRECTIONS: Match each form of address with its correct meaning.

_____ 1. Miss   a. used to address a married or an unmarried woman

_____ 2. Mr.   b. used to address a married woman

_____ 3. Mrs.   c. used to address a man

_____ 4. Ms.   d. used to address an unmarried woman

B. DIRECTIONS: Fill in the blank with the correct form of address.

Mr.   Ms.   Mrs.   Miss

1. Our mailman, _____ Bishop, had an accident.

2. My mother's name is _____ Matilde Smith.

3. Her sister, _____ Peggy Allen, will be getting married soon.

4. I do not know if she is married because she signs her name

   as _____ .

5. _____ George is a good mountain climber.

6. Young women use the _____ form of address.

7. Nat's mother is _____ Anglin.

8. The tennis champion, _____ Ritz, is the mother of four boys.

9. Our principal, _____ Steve Red, lives on Fifth Avenue.

10. The new teacher is _____ Louise Hebert, and she is not married.

VOCABULARY   **B. Word Meaning**   **1. d.** Forms of address

DIRECTIONS: Place the correct title in front of the following names.

Mr.   Mrs.   Miss

1. _____ Joe Haynes

2. _____ Joy Brooks (married)

3. _____ Therese Allen (unmarried)

4. _____ Dan Wright

5. _____ Lois Curtis (married)

6. _____ Pete Curtis

7. _____ Vivian Walker (unmarried)

8. _____ Sandra Jones (married)

9. _____ George Gobrecht

10. _____ Kim Lee (unmarried)

11. _____ Tracy Johnson (to be married)

12. _____ Robert Frank

VOCABULARY   B. Word Meaning   1. d. Forms of address

DIRECTIONS: Read the sentences carefully. Select the form of address that best fits into each sentence and write it in the blank.

1. The repairman, _____ Luke Bryant, stopped the leak.
   Miss   Mrs.   Mr.

2. When a woman marries, her title changes to _____.
   Miss   Mrs.   Mr.

3. The carpenter's name is _____ Ray Jones.
   Miss   Mrs.   Mr.

4. We could not tell if she was married since she signed her name

   _____ Ora Speed.
   Mrs.   Mr.   Ms.

5. _____ Jerome Hayes is a grandfather.
   Mr.   Mrs.   Miss

6. The unmarried teacher is _____ Joyce Flowers.
   Mr.   Mrs.   Miss

7. _____ Ruth Brown has three grandchildren.
   Mrs.   Miss   Mr.

8. The winner of the cake baking contest was the fireman's wife,

   _____ Sally Hill.
   Miss   Mr.   Mrs.

9. Our milkman, _____ David Gray, broke his leg.
   Ms.   Mr.   Mrs.

10. _____ Margo Ash was the first unmarried woman reporter.
    Miss   Mr.   Mrs.

11. _____ can be used by all women.
    Ms.   Mrs.   Mr.

12. _____ Cecile Coper will marry her boss.
    Miss   Mr.   Mrs.

VOCABULARY   **B. Word Meaning**   **1. e.** Career words

DIRECTIONS: Match each career word with the type of work involved.

_____ 1. artist

_____ 2. factory

_____ 3. lawyer

_____ 4. mechanic

_____ 5. nurse

_____ 6. office worker

_____ 7. teacher

_____ 8. vocation

_____ 9. training

_____ 10. operator

_____ 11. money

a. repairs automobiles

b. types letters, answers telephone

c. creates things with clay, paint, and other materials

d. runs a machine

e. preparing for a trade

f. helps students learn

g. handles legal business

h. an occupation, business, or trade

i. banking

j. building where things are made

k. cares for the ill

VOCABULARY   B. Word Meaning   1. e. Career words

DIRECTIONS: Select the best word to complete the sentence and write the word in the blank.

1. A _____ may work in hospitals.
         lawyer   factory   nurse

2. A banker handles _____ .
         money   mechanic   teacher

3. The _____ was busy in the courtroom.
         artist   lawyer   teacher

4. The painting was done by a good _____ .
         lawyer   teacher   artist

5. The _____ makes parts for television sets.
         lawyer   factory   teacher

6. The car was repaired by a very good _____ .
         mechanic   nurse   lawyer

7. His _____ as a writer is fun.
         mechanic   vocation   operator

8. The first grade _____ is a man.
         vocation   training   teacher

9. Tim is in _____ to be a TV camera operator.
         office   training   operator

10. The telephone _____ was very busy.
          artist   training   operator

11. All the phones were busy in the _____ .
          office   operator   money

12. A bank is a place to save _____ .
          money   artist   nurse

VOCABULARY   **B. Word Meaning**   **1. e.** Career words

DIRECTIONS: Match each career word with a phrase that relates to it.

_____ 1. A place where things are made

_____ 2. Makes bread and cakes

_____ 3. Writes legal papers

_____ 4. Helps students to learn

_____ 5. Paints, draws, creates beautiful art

_____ 6. Gives medicine to a sick person

_____ 7. Runs a machine to make something
or to keep something running

_____ 8. A place where a secretary works

_____ 9. An airplane repairperson

_____ 10. Used to buy goods

a. teacher

b. operator

c. office

d. nurse

e. money

f. mechanic

g. lawyer

h. factory

i. artist

j. baker

VOCABULARY   B. Word Meaning   1. e. Career words

DIRECTIONS: **Select the word that best completes the sentence and write the word in the blank.**

artist   teacher   lawyer   nurse

1. The _____ sold his painting to the museum.

2. A _____ is needed to help him get out of jail.

3. The _____ gave the sick woman some medicine.

4. Joe's dad is a science _____ at Bailey School.

5. An _____ can work with clay, oil paints, watercolors, and other media.

money   mechanic   factory   vocation

6. A _____ is the work or career one chooses.

7. The Simmons _____ makes transistors for computers.

8. The _____ checked the spark plugs in my car.

9. We use _____ to buy and trade goods.

10. The _____ repaired the engine in a few minutes.

training   office   operator   factory

11. The transistor clock had to be returned to the _____ for repairs.

12. The lift _____ works from 8 AM to 5 PM every day.

13. To be good at a job, you must get the necessary _____.

14. The president of the Walton Company is in his _____.

15. The doctor received her _____ at the Heart Center in Dallas.

A. DIRECTIONS: Match the color word with the correct object.

_____ 1. brown   a. bushes

_____ 2. green   b. royalty

_____ 3. orange   c. leather

_____ 4. purple   d. pumpkin

B. DIRECTIONS: Circle the item that is not the color stated.

1. green   — stems,   crackers,   grass,   leaves
2. brown   — leather,   horse,   shoes,   snow
3. orange — carrot,   ghost,   flower,   pumpkin
4. purple — flower,   grass,   rug,   curtain
5. green   — curtains,   crayons,   shoes,   sand
6. orange — pumpkins,   cards,   rain,   blouse
7. brown   — cat,   butter,   dog,   trousers
8. purple — vanilla ice cream,   chair,   pen,   paper

VOCABULARY   B. Word Meaning   1. f. Color words

DIRECTIONS: Read the phrases and write <u>Yes</u> if you think such a colored thing is possible. Write <u>No</u> if you think such a colored thing is not likely.

_____ 1. a purple cow

_____ 2. a brown tree trunk

_____ 3. a purple sweater

_____ 4. an orange onion

_____ 5. a green lamb

_____ 6. a brown Christmas tree

_____ 7. a green bush

_____ 8. purple grass

_____ 9. a brown football

_____ 10. a green cat

_____ 11. an orange grape

_____ 12. a green door

VOCABULARY   B. Word Meaning   1. f. Color words

A. DIRECTIONS: Write <u>Yes</u> in front of the sentence if you think it is likely to be true or likely to happen. Write <u>No</u> in front of the sentence if you think it is unlikely to be true or to happen.

_____   1. The purple road to school was two miles long.

_____   2. The ground was covered with four inches of green snow.

_____   3. The trees were covered with budding green leaves.

_____   4. My brown shoes need polishing.

_____   5. The teacher wrote on the orange board with yellow chalk.

_____   6. Liz has a purple skirt.

_____   7. The purple chocolate candy bar costs 25¢.

_____   8. The sun is brown.

_____   9. The orange door was locked.

_____   10. Mom sat in the brown chair.

_____   11. The house had a green gate.

_____   12. The orange apples made a good pie.

B. DIRECTIONS: Underline the color words in the above sentences.

A. DIRECTIONS: Match each word with its correct meaning.

_____ 1. centigrade

a. metric measure of length

_____ 2. gram

b. a measure of temperature

_____ 3. liter

c. metric measure of volume

_____ 4. meter

d. metric measure of weight

B. DIRECTIONS: Read the following list of ten items. Decide how each item would be measured in the metric system and write the measuring term in the blank next to the item.

centigrade   gram   liter   meter

1. ribbon   _____

2. apple juice   _____

3. pork chops   _____

4. fabric   _____

5. temperature in room   _____

6. fruit punch   _____

7. hot dogs   _____

8. lace   _____

9. pigs' feet   _____

10. outdoor temperature   _____

VOCABULARY   B. Word Meaning   1. g. Metric words

DIRECTIONS: Fill in the correct metric word for each of the following sentences.

centigrade   gram   liter   meter

1. The temperature yesterday was 20° _____ .

2. The cake recipe called for two _____(s) of baking soda.

3. The shirt was made from one _____ of silk.

4. Mother bought a _____ of milk.

5. The children quickly drank the _____ of fruit juice.

6. He could only eat a few _____(s) of meat at a time.

7. I have a Fahrenheit thermometer, not a _____ one.

8. He had driven only ten _____(s) before the car broke down.

9. You buy cheese by the _____ .

10. She jumped three and a half _____(s) in the track meet.

VOCABULARY   B. Word Meaning   1. g. Metric words

DIRECTIONS: In the blank, write the correct metric term to measure each of the following items.

centigrade   meter   gram   liter

1. oil   _____

2. meat   _____

3. tablecloth   _____

4. orange juice   _____

5. temperature in an oven   _____

6. bread   _____

7. tallness of a person   _____

8. miles traveled   _____

9. freezer temperature   _____

10. gasoline   _____

11. size of a table   _____

12. package of raisins   _____

VOCABULARY   **B. Word Meaning**   **1. h.** Curriculum words

DIRECTIONS: Place each word in the correct column.

add	country	ecology	even
American	fall	few	greater
less	number	odd	seasons
set	space	spring	state
subtract	summer	United States	winter
world			

Arithmetic	Science	History (Social Studies)
_____	_____	_____
_____	_____	_____
_____	_____	_____
_____	_____	_____
_____	_____	_____
_____	_____	_____
_____	_____	_____
_____	_____	_____

VOCABULARY   B. Word Meaning   1. h. Curriculum words

DIRECTIONS: Circle the word under each of the following sentences that completes the sentence correctly.

1. A way to get six is to _____ five and one.
   winter   add   set

2. The _____ flag is red, white, and blue.
   even   ecology   American

3. The United States is one _____.
   greater   less   country

4. _____ is the science that deals with the relation of living things to their surroundings and to each other.
   Ecology   Country   American

5. Two, four, and six are _____ numbers.
   few   even   odd

6. Leaves change their colors in the _____.
   seasons   fall   add

7. Give me a _____ marbles.
   add   space   few

8. Twelve is _____ than ten.
   greater   less   number

9. Which _____ follows fourteen?
   subtract   odd   number

10. Give Leroy two _____ than six.
    spring   less   even

11. The opposite of an even number is a number that is _____.
    odd   set   space

12. There are four _____ in the year.
    spring   seasons   fall

VOCABULARY   **B. Word Meaning**   **1. h.** Curriculum words

DIRECTIONS: In the blank in each sentence, write the word that completes the sentence correctly.

1. The children asked, "Is the _____ round?"
   add   world   American

2. I think of snow and ice when you say the word _____.
   spring   fall   winter

3. The 50 states make up the _____.
   United States   state   seasons

4. _____ means no school and fun times.
       Summer   State   Few

5. When you _____, the answer is the remainder.
   fall   subtract   add

6. In which _____ do you live?
   set   summer   state

7. The Easter season is in the _____.
   summer   winter   spring

8. The air _____ over the airport is crowded.
   spring   space   world

9. Give me a _____ of numbers that make up six.
   set   few   number

10. Six feet is _____ than three feet.
    even   greater   less

11. Three, five, and seven are _____ numbers.
    country   even   odd

12. _____ comes before summer.
       Seasons   Spring   State

VOCABULARY   B. Word Meaning   1. h. Curriculum words

DIRECTIONS: Choose the correct word to complete each sentence and write the word in the blank.

number   less   odd   subtract

1. Write the _____ that comes after 77.

2. Sixty is _____ than a hundred.

3. Seven is an _____ number.

4. To take one number away from another is to _____.

country   American   world   state

5. Rhode Island is the smallest _____ in the nation.

6. Paul Revere is an _____ hero.

7. Poland is a _____ in Europe.

8. He flew around the _____ in ten days.

winter   even   few   season

9. Which _____ follows summer?

10. Bears hibernate in the _____.

11. Adding six and six will give you an _____ number.

12. Only a _____ girls are six feet tall.

VOCABULARY   **B. Word Meaning**   **1. h.** Curriculum words   53

DIRECTIONS: Choose the correct word to complete each sentence and write the word in the blank.

add   ecology   fall   greater

1. Please _____ some salt to the soup.

2. Circle the number _____ _____ than ten.

3. The science of _____ is important.

4. Leaves change color in the _____.

set   space   spring   summer

5. There is much time to play in the _____.

6. The number _____ was incorrect.

7. Everyone needs his or her own _____.

8. Many flowers bloom in the _____.

United States   season   greater   subtract

9. I am proud to live in the _____.

10. Schools are closed during the Christmas _____.

11. Please _____ ten points from your score.

12. Forty is _____ than twenty.

WORD ANALYSIS   A. 1. *Initial consonant sounds*

DIRECTIONS: Match each word with its beginning sound.

Part A.

1. kite   _____ t

2. bucks   _____ g

3. tea   _____ y

4. monkey   _____ d

5. young   _____ c

6. gallop   _____ b

7. X-ray   _____ n

8. drag   _____ k

9. neck   _____ x

10. cook   _____ m

Part B.

1. wind   _____ r

2. jam   _____ v

3. rock   _____ z

4. queer   _____ j

5. visit   _____ l

6. horses   _____ w

7. zoo   _____ f

8. face   _____ p

9. lamp   _____ h

10. pants   _____ q

WORD ANALYSIS   A.   1. *Initial consonant sounds*

DIRECTIONS: Select the consonant sound needed to begin each word.

Group A.   b   v   f   w   s

1. ___isit   2. ___ence   3. ___orld   4. ___ark   5. ___eat

Group B.   h   c   g   r   z

1. ___up   2. ___elp   3. ___oose   4. ___ero   5. ___abbit

Group C.   v   d   y   m   k

1. ___est   2. ___ellow   3. ___ull   4. ___ess   5. ___itten

Group D.   p   n   l   y   j

1. ___ail   2. ___uggle   3. ___ut   4. ___ou   5. ___ace

WORD ANALYSIS   A. 1. *Initial consonant sounds*

DIRECTIONS: Find three words from the list that begin with the same consonant blend.

1. gl   _____   _____   _____

2. br   _____   _____   _____

3. sm   _____   _____   _____

4. gr   _____   _____   _____

5. fr   _____   _____   _____

branch	from	glow
smile	grove	fresh
glass	smack	ground
green	bring	brook
friend	glen	smug

WORD ANALYSIS   A. 1. *Initial consonant sounds*

DIRECTIONS: Match the consonant blend with the picture that begins with the blend sound.

1. cr

___

a.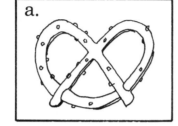

g.

7. sn

___

2. bl

___

b.

h.

8. cl

___

3. th

___

c.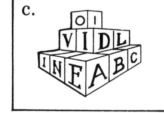

i.

9. st

___

4. pr

___

d.

j.

10. pl

___

5. dr

___

e.

k.

11. wh

___

6. sh

___

f.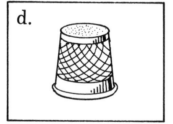

l.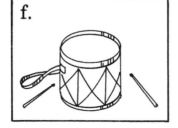

12. ch

___

A. DIRECTIONS: Underline the word or words in each line that begin with the same consonant blend as the first word.

1. <u>str</u>ange   stoop   struck   sand

2. <u>chr</u>ome   chose   chunk   christen

3. <u>sch</u>ool   scope   schedule   scarf

4. <u>spl</u>atter   splint   spoil   spot

5. <u>thr</u>ead   throne   thin   three

6. <u>spr</u>ing   sponge   spree   spoke

B. DIRECTIONS: Use one of the blends in each example to make a word. Write the blend in front of the word.

7. str
    sch _____ ong
    spr

8. Spl
    Spr _____ istmas
    Chr

9. spr
    thr _____ one
    chr

10. sch
    thr _____ ool
    chr

11. str
    spr _____ ee
    chr

12. spl
    chr _____ ash
    sch

C. DIRECTIONS: Read the sentences carefully and choose the word that best completes each sentence. Write the correct word on the line.

13. The water in the _____ was good to drink.
    spring   swing   thing

14. The _____ boys went for a swim.
    treat   tree   three

15. The _____ of light moved across the sky.
    straw   steam   stray

16. The capsule _____ down on Tuesday.
    splashed   sponged   spurted

17. The _____ was two miles from home.
    scat   scan   school

18. The _____ tree was decorated with red balls.
    Christmas   Church   Chime

WORD ANALYSIS   A. 1. *Initial consonant sounds*

DIRECTIONS: Choose a consonant or consonant blend in each example to make a word. Write the consonant or blend in front of the word.

1. ch
    sh   _____ eck
    dr

2. gr
    sm   _____ ound
    spr

3. f
    j   _____ obile
    m

4. v
    pl   _____ ank
    chr

5. l
    th   _____ in
    st

6. sn
    st   _____ anket
    bl

7. sw
    fl   _____ an
    gl

8. q
    th   _____ ick
    pl

9. chr
    k   _____ ump
    sl

10. sp
    str   _____ ill
    y

11. spl
    f   _____ own
    br

12. k
    l   _____ eave
    b

13. c
    j   _____ abin
    n

14. t
    x   _____ eeth
    d

15. j
    p   _____ itten
    k

16. spr
    str   _____ ing
    thr

17. w
    f   _____ olf
    y

18. th
    sn   _____ iff
    cl

19. f
    w   _____ ox
    j

20. k
    b   _____ anch
    r

WORD ANALYSIS   A.   2. *Short and long vowel sounds*

DIRECTIONS: Read each word carefully and listen to the vowel sound. Write the letter that makes the vowel sound beside each word. Then write long beside the letter if the vowel sound is long, and short beside the letter if the vowel sound is short.

1. nod   _____   _____

2. shine   _____   _____

3. blast   _____   _____

4. right   _____   _____

5. cast   _____   _____

6. back   _____   _____

7. hide   _____   _____

8. kick   _____   _____

9. pull   _____   _____

10. gray   _____   _____

11. jump   _____   _____

12. made   _____   _____

13. bone   _____   _____

14. mule   _____   _____

15. nest   _____   _____

16. beet   _____   _____

17. top   _____   _____

18. red   _____   _____

19. sled   _____   _____

20. stove   _____   _____

A. DIRECTIONS: Read the list of words. Fill in the sentences by choosing a word with a short vowel sound.

get	until	lick	stove	doll	wet	most
till	find	nice	neck	best	own	half
chin	shut	wag	pick	set	stick	

1. Duke the dog wanted to _____ out of the doghouse.

2. Duke had to wait _____ Clancy, another dog, got out first.

3. Duke would _____ his tail when he was fed.

4. The door to the playhouse was _____.

5. Nancy helped to _____ berries.

6. The ground is _____ because it rained.

7. Dick won a prize for drawing the _____ picture.

8. Dogs like to _____ your hands.

9. The children had fun playing with the _____ house.

10. Sarah put a woolen scarf around her _____.

B. DIRECTIONS: Read each sentence and fill in the blank by choosing a word with a long vowel sound.

1. He played a tune on my _____.	bugle	duck	brush
2. Ice _____ make soda cold.	cut	cubes	duke
3. The _____ doll had blue eyes.	small	such	cute
4. Elephants are _____.	huge	curb	tune
5. The _____ made a buzzing sound.	tree	bee	tea
6. A _____ is a cousin of a king.	duke	duck	doe
7. At the zoo we saw some _____.	tigers	times	find
8. The lion seemed very _____.	tile	wild	child
9. The white bears at the zoo came from a _____ country.	mold	hold	cold
10. The panda _____ over.	smoke	pole	rolled

WORD ANALYSIS   A. 2. *Short and long vowel sounds*

DIRECTIONS: Say each word silently. If the vowel that you hear is long, write the word in the column under long; if it is short, write the word in the column under short.

	Long	**Short**
1. best	_____	_____
2. bare	_____	_____
3. king	_____	_____
4. key	_____	_____
5. bad	_____	_____
6. like	_____	_____
7. clock	_____	_____
8. inn	_____	_____
9. pole	_____	_____
10. shape	_____	_____
11. thing	_____	_____
12. bug	_____	_____
13. baked	_____	_____
14. mum	_____	_____
15. trust	_____	_____

WORD ANALYSIS   A. 2. *Short and long vowel sounds*

DIRECTIONS: Some words have more than one vowel sound. Say the following words silently. Write on the line the vowel sound you hear in the underlined part of the word and tell if the vowel sound is long or short.

Example:

forget ___e___ ___short___

1. peanut _____ _____

2. hobby _____ _____

3. sandwich _____ _____

4. greet _____ _____

5. number _____ _____

6. secret _____ _____

7. dropped _____ _____

8. rodeo _____ _____

9. slate _____ _____

10. package _____ _____

11. nicely _____ _____

12. plotting _____ _____

13. Utah _____ _____

14. gritting _____ _____

15. desert _____ _____

WORD ANALYSIS   A. 2. *Short and long vowel sounds*

DIRECTIONS: Read the first word in each line, paying attention to the vowel sound. Circle the word in the line that has the same long or short vowel sound.

1. pet	bear	steer	fed
2. gum	hum	glue	tube
3. ice	dim	tip	like
4. toe	top	look	go
5. cut	nut	guide	purple
6. game	star	land	same
7. dike	limb	rice	lift
8. lad	gate	mail	pad
9. music	mutt	dull	due
10. bold	more	fold	wood
11. rake	half	hate	sat
12. snow	so	some	sore
13. sum	dupe	lung	murk
14. rid	five	pig	size
15. key	seed	wear	rest

WORD ANALYSIS   A.   3. a. Adding *s, es, d, ed, ing, er, est*

DIRECTIONS: Fill the blanks in these sentences by placing the proper ending on the word at the end of the sentence. Choose from the following list of endings.

s   es   d   ed   ing   er   est

1. The girls were _____ down the lane.   walk

2. Nothing seemed _____ than the candy canes.   sweet

3. The _____ were covered with mud.   shoe

4. Nathan has two white _____.   rabbit

5. December 21 is the _____ day of the year.   short

6. The bird kept _____.   sing

7. We listened to the bell _____ as we came to school.   ring

8. The boy _____ as he walked past the cemetery.   whistle

9. _____ change the meanings of words.   suffix

10. The children _____ water out of the tub onto the bathroom floor.   splash

11. The fur _____ gave the Indians necklaces and mirrors.   trader

12. Jeff fed _____ to the mule.   carrot

13. Peter is the _____ of four boys in his family.   tall

14. The baker _____ the dough into a squirrel.   shape

15. Goblins and _____ stirred about.   witch

16. The cat was _____ as I stroked him.   purr

17. The dentist _____ Jane's two front teeth.   pull

18. Andrew roller _____ from his house to the store.   skate

19. It takes many _____ to make a yard.   inch

20. Mary _____ her friends to the puppet show.   invite

WORD ANALYSIS   A. 3. a. Adding *s, es, d, ed, ing, er, est*

DIRECTIONS: Identify the root word by drawing a circle around the ending that was added to the word.

1. cows	11. wanted
2. sooner	12. stitches
3. marches	13. darkest
4. wilder	14. greener
5. fastest	15. bottled
6. goats	16. candles
7. spending	17. marching
8. louder	18. excited
9. pitches	19. belonged
10. marking	20. nearest

WORD ANALYSIS   **A. 3. a.** Adding *s, es, d, ed, ing, er, est*

DIRECTIONS: Write the word that fits best in each sentence.

1. Grandmother has four _____ and ten kittens in the barn.

cat   cats   cates

2. Is Superman the _____ man?

fast   faster   fastest

3. The big _____ cat crossed my path.

blackest   black   blacker

4. Dad bought a basket of white _____.

grapes   grape   grapest

5. Mutt is _____ than Jeff.

lean   leaner   leanest

6. The bush near the door is _____ than the others.

larger   large   largest

7. John _____ with joy as he opened the package.

exclaim   exclaimed   exclaims

8. _____ the salty water made Marc sick.

Drink   Drinker   Drinking

9. Ann _____ her pennies over and over again.

count   counted   counting

10. The cowboy _____ for his gun to kill the snake.

reached   reach   reaching

11. The girls _____ playing with their dolls yesterday.

enjoy   enjoyed   enjoying

12. During the flood, all of the _____ were filled with water.

ditch   ditches   ditching

13. The teacher _____ that the class was quiet.

note   noted   noting

14. The maid _____ the children while Mother worked.

mind   minded   minding

15. The artist _____ the sunset.

paint   painting   painted

16. Who is _____ at the door?

knock   knockest   knocking

A. DIRECTIONS: Some words drop the final <u>e</u> before adding <u>ing</u>. Change these words to <u>ing</u> words.

1. chase　　　　　　　_____

2. wave　　　　　　　_____

3. smile　　　　　　　_____

4. invite　　　　　　　_____

5. place　　　　　　　_____

6. slide　　　　　　　_____

7. smoke　　　　　　　_____

8. freeze　　　　　　　_____

9. give　　　　　　　_____

10. become　　　　　　_____

B. DIRECTIONS: An ending has been added to these words. Write the root word on the line.

1. wiggling　　　　　　_____

2. parading　　　　　　_____

3. biking　　　　　　　_____

4. choking　　　　　　_____

5. whistling　　　　　_____

6. behaving　　　　　　_____

7. glancing　　　　　　_____

8. squeezing　　　　　_____

9. forcing　　　　　　_____

10. hiding　　　　　　　_____

WORD ANALYSIS   A.   3. b.   Dropping final *e* and adding *ing*

DIRECTIONS: Circle the correct root word for the first word of every line.

1. hating   a. hat   b. hate   c. ha

2. believing   a. believe   b. believ   c. belie

3. dancing   a. dan   b. danc   c. dance

4. facing   a. face   b. fac   c. fa

5. curing   a. cur   b. cure   c. cu

6. urging   a. ur   b. urg   c. urge

7. relating   a. relate   b. relat   c. rela

8. capturing   a. capt   b. capture   c. captur

9. inviting   a. invite   b. invit   c. invi

10. writing   a. writ   b. write   c. writin

11. solving   a. solve   b. solvin   c. solv

12. voicing   a. voice   b. voic   c. voicin

13. poling   a. pol   b. po   c. pole

14. shaking   a. sha   b. shake   c. shak

15. prizing   a. prizi   b. prize   c. priz

WORD ANALYSIS   **A.**   **3. a.** Adding *s, es, d, ed, ing, er, est*
                       b. Dropping final *e* and adding *ing*

DIRECTIONS: There is an underlined word in every sentence. Using what you know about word endings, circle the root word of the underlined word in every sentence.

1. The football game was very <u>exciting</u>.
   excit   excite   excitin

2. The cat <u>dozes</u> by the fire.
   dozes   doze   doz

3. The birds <u>chattered</u> in the early hours of the morning.
   chatter   chat   chattere

4. Jane does not like to eat <u>eggs</u>.
   eg   egg   eggs

5. Dad <u>agreed</u> to take the girls fishing.
   agr   agree   agre

6. The clown was <u>wobbling</u> on his bicycle.
   wobb   wobble   wobblin

7. The <u>sharpest</u> knife was used to cut the rope.
   sharpe   shar   sharp

8. The pink baskets were <u>taller</u> than the white ones.
   tal   tall   talle

9. <u>Watching</u> the monkeys was fun.
   watch   watchin   watc

10. Who likes to wash the <u>dishes</u>?
    dish   dishe   dishes

11. Ann's dog <u>jumped</u> over the gate.
    jum   jumpe   jump

12. "Put a <u>heading</u> on your paper," said the teacher.
    head   headin   headi

13. I <u>expected</u> Grandpa to come to the party.
    expecte   expect   expec

14. The <u>fastest</u> car won the race.
    faste   fast   fas

15. The <u>greater</u> amount of rice was used for the pudding.
    great   greate   grea

16. When the rain began, Dad <u>closed</u> the window.
    clo   clos   close

WORD ANALYSIS   **A.** **3.** **a.** Adding *s, es, d, ed, ing, er, est*
                        b. Dropping final *e* and adding *ing*

DIRECTIONS: Read the following words and write the root word of each in the blank.

1. blades   _____

2. roller   _____

3. pieced   _____

4. answered   _____

5. freezing   _____

6. braced   _____

7. pinches   _____

8. boats   _____

9. softest   _____

10. tester   _____

11. muttering   _____

12. moving   _____

13. hibernating   _____

14. acorns   _____

15. honking   _____

16. proudest   _____

17. stitches   _____

18. cleaned   _____

19. united   _____

20. quicker   _____

WORD ANALYSIS   **A. 3. a.** Adding *s, es, d, ed, ing, er, est*
                          b. Dropping final *e* and adding *ing*

DIRECTIONS: Fill in the blanks by placing the proper ending on the word at the end of the sentence. Choose from the following list of endings.

s   es   d   ed   ing   er   est

1. Greg is the _____ of the band.   lead

2. The _____ soldier saved the baby.   brave

3. Marguerite was _____ for a horse.   wish

4. Chuck and Will are _____.   friend

5. The _____ girl in the class won the prize.   short

6. The sign read, No _____.   smoke

7. The dog _____ around the room looking for Jane.   sniff

8. The twins _____ home to tell Dad the news.   race

9. The farmer mended the four _____.   fence

10. The two _____ were made of gold.   brush

11. Who do you think has the _____ dog?   smart

12. Our team _____ over the finish line.   rush

13. The clown _____ the little man into the air.   lift

14. The train kept _____ down the track.   move

15. Mr. Smith used a _____ to paint the room.   roll

16. Hungry boys were _____ the cookies.   pocket

17. The postman _____ the letter yesterday.   stamp

18. The deep-_____ man said, "Stop."   voice

19. Jim _____ his shoes last week.   shine

20. The fairy told the boy to make three _____.   wish

WORD ANALYSIS   **A.   3. a.** Adding *s, es, d, ed, ing, er, est*
                        b. Dropping final *e* and adding *ing*

DIRECTIONS: Make as many new words as possible by adding the endings s̲, e̲s̲, d̲, ed, i̲n̲g̲, e̲r̲, and e̲s̲t̲ to the following root words.

1. add   _____, _____, _____,
   _____

2. spread   _____, _____, _____

3. vine   _____

4. spell   _____, _____, _____,
   _____

5. sink   _____, _____, _____

6. grand   _____, _____

7. melt   _____, _____, _____

8. make   _____, _____, _____

9. high   _____, _____

10. light   _____, _____, _____,
    _____, _____

11. bare   _____, _____, _____,
    _____, _____

12. block   _____, _____, _____,
    _____

13. calm   _____, _____, _____,
    _____, _____

14. suppose _____, _____, _____

15. imagine _____, _____, _____

16. book   _____, _____, _____

DIRECTIONS: Underline the root word.

1. kisses

2. needed

3. stroked

4. reached

5. tighter

6. smartest

7. passing

8. taxes

9. twisting

10. fists

11. nicest

12. bending

13. eels

14. puzzled

15. bikes

16. weaker

17. counted

18. dearest

19. forced

20. warning

WORD ANALYSIS **A. 3. c.** Doubling the consonant before adding *ing*

DIRECTIONS: Form a new word by adding the suffix <u>ing</u> to these words. Remember that in some words you must double the consonant before adding <u>ing</u>.

1. wag _____
9. spot _____

2. grin _____
10. grab _____

3. slip _____
11. strip _____

4. thin _____
12. hop _____

5. sled _____
13. stop _____

6. rub _____
14. cut _____

7. rap _____
15. pop _____

8. skin _____
16. swim _____

WORD ANALYSIS   A. 3. c. Doubling the consonant before adding *ing*

DIRECTIONS: Write the root word for each word in the following list.

1. fitting _____

2. nodding _____

3. running _____

4. ripping _____

5. napping _____

6. stripping _____

7. sitting _____

8. shopping _____

9. shedding _____

10. penning _____

11. stirring _____

12. canning _____

13. propelling _____

14. chopping _____

15. fanning _____

WORD ANALYSIS   **A. 3. c.** Doubling the consonant before adding *ing*

DIRECTIONS: There is an underlined word in every sentence. Using what you know about word endings, circle the root word of the underlined word in every sentence.

1. Nellie was busy <u>filling</u> the bucket with berries.
   fil   fill   fille

2. The new puppy was <u>licking</u> my fingers.
   licki   lic   lick

3. Ann was <u>leaning</u> against the fence.
   lean   lea   leani

4. Paul is <u>getting</u> some apples.
   gett   get   getti

5. Margo was <u>dragging</u> the wagon full of papers.
   dragg   draggi   drag

6. The red flag is a <u>warning</u> flag.
   warn   war   warni

7. The urchin was <u>begging</u> for food.
   beg   begg   be

8. The pony was <u>trotting</u> around the track.
   trott   trot   trotti

9. Grandpa was <u>padding</u> around the house in his slippers.
   pad   padd   pa

10. The boys reached out and were <u>grabbing</u> for the rope.
    grabb   grabbi   grab

11. The seal enjoyed <u>flipping</u> the ball.
    flipp   flip   fli

12. The <u>winning</u> team had an ice cream party.
    win   winn   winni

13. The fish was <u>flopping</u> on the deck.
    flopp   flop   flo

14. The boy was <u>bedding</u> down for the night.
    bed   bedd   be

15. The <u>jutting</u> pier made docking the boat dangerous.
    jut   jutti   jutt

WORD ANALYSIS   A. 3. c. Doubling the consonant before adding *ing*

DIRECTIONS: Make new words from this list of words by adding ing.

1. beg   _____

2. hem   _____

3. swim   _____

4. gum   _____

5. chum   _____

6. bog   _____

7. chug   _____

8. can   _____

9. blot   _____

10. bob   _____

11. net   _____

12. slip   _____

13. plan   _____

14. span   _____

15. slam   _____

WORD ANALYSIS   A. 3. c. Doubling the consonant before adding *ing*

DIRECTIONS: Read the sentence and the word at the beginning of the sentence. Write the correct <u>ing</u> form of the word on the line.

hem   1. Mother was _____ Kathryn's dress.
             hemming   heming

pin   2. The machine was _____ the fabric to the board.
             pining   pinning

chug   3. The train came _____ along.
             chugging   chuging

sit   4. Greg and Andy were _____ on the fence.
             sitting   siting

hug   5. The little girl enjoys _____ her doll.
             hugging   huging

strip   6. The boys were _____ the old paint off the wagon.
             stripping   striping

bag   7. _____ groceries is a way to earn money.
             Baging   Bagging

rip   8. As he jumped over the fence, he heard a _____ sound.
             ripping   riping

chop   9. The farmer is _____ wood for his fireplace.
             chopping   choping

clip   10. The barber was _____ the young man's hair.
             cliping   clipping

skim   11. The skater seemed to be _____ over the ice.
             skimming   skiming

slap   12. I love the _____ sound of water against the pier.
             slapping   slaping

wrap   13. The girls giggled as they were _____ the gifts.
             wrapping   wraping

WORD ANALYSIS   **A. 3. d.** Changing *y* to *i* before adding *es*

DIRECTIONS: Circle the form of the word that should be used.

1. The baby crys / cries / cris when he is hungry.

2. The hungry baby / babies / babis were fed at noon.

3. The bodies / body / bodis of the soldiers were brought home.

4. The kite flies / fly / flis well.

5. In the fifty / fifties / fiftis, Elvis Presley was popular.

6. Nyette visited many countris / country / countries last year.

7. Her grandfather was born in the eighteen nineties / ninetys / ninetis.

8. Many library / librarys / libraries are closed on holidays.

9. On Sunday, I enjoy reading the funnys / funnies / funnis.

10. The factory / factories / factoris were closed on Thanksgiving Day.

11. The nine puppis / puppys / puppies nestled close to their mother.

12. Sam went to three birthday partys / parties / partis.

13. Mother dries / dry / drys her clothes by hanging them outdoors.

14. John hurrys / hurries / hurris to school because he likes to be on time.

15. The cook fry / fries / frys the eggs.

WORD ANALYSIS   A. 3. d. Changing *y* to *i* before adding *es*

DIRECTIONS: From the following list of words, choose the word that best completes each sentence and write it in the blank.

spies	buggies
pries	fries
flies	tries
dries	carries
ponies	studies

1. Susan _____ into my affairs.

2. That pan is used when Mother _____ potatoes.

3. Marc _____ hard to be a good student in school.

4. The robin _____ south for the winter.

5. Mother _____ the baby after her bath.

6. The young man _____ the packages for the elderly woman.

7. The report card showed that his _____ suffered during the holidays.

8. The three _____ looked beautiful as they ran around the pasture.

9. The ladies were taken to the party in fancy _____.

10. The FBI _____ on gangsters.

WORD ANALYSIS   A. 3. d. Changing *y* to *i* before adding *es*

DIRECTIONS: Write the root word for each of the following.

1. pries   _____

2. dries   _____

3. stories   _____

4. colonies   _____

5. flies   _____

6. worries   _____

7. skies   _____

8. hurries   _____

9. families   _____

10. butterflies   _____

11. carries   _____

12. berries   _____

13. hobbies   _____

14. pennies   _____

15. twenties   _____

WORD ANALYSIS   A. 3. d. Changing *y* to *i* before adding *es*

DIRECTIONS: Fill the blank in each sentence by using the correct form of the word at the end of the sentence.

1. Larry _____ to be a brave boy when he goes to the dentist.   try

2. Many _____ buzzed around the room and they were a nuisance.   fly

3. Grandpa enjoys telling _____ to his grandchildren.   story

4. The man _____ all of the milk cartons into a large can.   empty

5. The children enjoyed chasing _____ in the park.   butterfly

6. The five _____ were soft and cuddly.   bunny

7. The man _____ the door open with a stick.   pry

8. The two _____ were identical.   pony

9. The _____ were delicious.   candy

10. The _____ were washed and added to the pie.   berry

11. The three _____ joined at one point.   county

12. The prince _____ the princess in the story.   marry

WORD ANALYSIS   **A. 3. d.** Changing *y* to *i* before adding *es*

DIRECTIONS: Circle the correct root word for each word in the first column.

1. posies	posy	posi
2. factories	factory	factori
3. skies	sky	ski
4. memories	memori	memory
5. candies	candy	candi
6. countries	countri	country
7. jellies	jelly	jelli
8. kitties	kitty	kitti
9. marries	marry	marri
10. cities	citi	city
11. carries	carry	carri
12. cherries	cherry	cherri
13. fifties	fifty	fifti
14. puppies	puppy	puppi
15. lullabies	lullaby	lullabi

WORD ANALYSIS **A.** **3.** **a.** Adding *s, es, d, ed, ing, er, est*
b. Dropping final *e* and adding *ing*
c. Doubling the consonant before adding *ing*
d. Changing *y* to *i* before adding *es*

DIRECTIONS: Mark the letter of the alphabet that tells what was done to the root word to make a new word and underline the root word.

a. Adding s̲, e̲s̲, d̲, e̲d̲, i̲n̲g̲, e̲r̲, e̲s̲t̲
b. Dropping final e̲ and adding ing̲
c. Doubling the consonant before adding ing
d. Changing y̲ to i̲ before adding e̲s̲

1. pennies _____ a _____ b _____ c _____ d

2. tables _____ a _____ b _____ c _____ d

3. picking _____ a _____ b _____ c _____ d

4. staging _____ a _____ b _____ c _____ d

5. leaving _____ a _____ b _____ c _____ d

6. trained _____ a _____ b _____ c _____ d

7. ladies _____ a _____ b _____ c _____ d

8. oldest _____ a _____ b _____ c _____ d

9. quieter _____ a _____ b _____ c _____ d

10. skies _____ a _____ b _____ c _____ d

11. closed _____ a _____ b _____ c _____ d

12. trapping _____ a _____ b _____ c _____ d

13. tolling _____ a _____ b _____ c _____ d

14. hurries _____ a _____ b _____ c _____ d

15. raising _____ a _____ b _____ c _____ d

WORD ANALYSIS   **A. 3. a.** Adding *s, es, d, ed, ing, er, est*
                 b. Dropping final *e* and adding *ing*
                 c. Doubling the consonant before adding *ing*
                 d. Changing *y* to *i* before adding *es*

DIRECTIONS: Write the root word for each of the following words.

1. tips   _____
2. started   _____
3. splashes   _____
4. shamed   _____
5. spreader   _____
6. vases   _____
7. talking   _____
8. swimming   _____
9. grinning   _____
10. tasting   _____

11. timing   _____
12. jetting   _____
13. forties   _____
14. thrashes   _____
15. shouted   _____
16. spaded   _____
17. rugs   _____
18. teller   _____
19. sharpest   _____
20. hurries   _____

WORD ANALYSIS   **A. 3. a.** Adding *s, es, d, ed, ing, er, est*
                          b. Dropping final *e* and adding *ing*
                          c. Doubling the consonant before adding *ing*
                          d. Changing *y* to *i* before adding *es*

DIRECTIONS: Make a new word by adding s, es, d, ed, ing, er, or est to each of the following root words.

1. blanket   _____

2. camp   _____

3. drag   _____

4. puppy   _____

5. sled   _____

6. jelly   _____

7. fry   _____

8. slim   _____

9. blaze   _____

10. boil   _____

11. pray   _____

12. twenty   _____

13. tape   _____

14. quit   _____

15. taste   _____

WORD ANALYSIS   **A. 3. a.** Adding *s, es, d, ed, ing, er, est*
                          b. Dropping final *e* and adding *ing*
                          c. Doubling the consonant before adding *ing*
                          d. Changing *y* to *i* before adding *es*

DIRECTIONS: Fill in the blanks by selecting the correct word under each sentence.

1. The lion was _____ about in his pen.
    run   running   runing

2. When the siren blew, Heidi _____.
    howl   howled   howls

3. Grandpa's plane was late in _____.
    departing   departting   depart

4. Dan is _____ at his shop.
    works   working   workking

5. Dad is the _____ person in our family.
    tallest   tall   talest

6. Grandma enjoys baking _____.
    cookies   cooky   cook

7. It _____ very hard last night.
    rained   rains   rain

8. The dentist would not let her eat _____.
    carrot   carrots   carrotest

9. Sandy _____ going to the movies.
    enjoys   enjoy   enjoying

10. Uncle Bob is _____ the newspaper.
    read   reades   reading

11. The girls _____ over the wall.
    leaps   leaped   leaping

12. Bess was _____ her eyes in the sunlight.
    blinks   blinked   blinking

WORD ANALYSIS   **A.** **3. a.** Adding *s, es, d, ed, ing, er, est*
                          b. Dropping final *e* and adding *ing*
                          c. Doubling the consonant before adding *ing*
                          d. Changing *y* to *i* before adding *es*

DIRECTIONS: Mark the letter of the alphabet that tells what was done to the root word.

a. Adding s, es, ed, ing, er, est
b. Dropping final e and adding ing
c. Doubling the consonant before adding ing
d. Changing y to i before adding es

1. pads   ____ a   ____ b   ____ c   ____ d

2. hearing   ____ a   ____ b   ____ c   ____ d

3. waved   ____ a   ____ b   ____ c   ____ d

4. shopping   ____ a   ____ b   ____ c   ____ d

5. tracking   ____ a   ____ b   ____ c   ____ d

6. tanning   ____ a   ____ b   ____ c   ____ d

7. crasher   ____ a   ____ b   ____ c   ____ d

8. foxes   ____ a   ____ b   ____ c   ____ d

9. brownest   ____ a   ____ b   ____ c   ____ d

10. stamper   ____ a   ____ b   ____ c   ____ d

11. paging   ____ a   ____ b   ____ c   ____ d

12. fined   ____ a   ____ b   ____ c   ____ d

13. jellies   ____ a   ____ b   ____ c   ____ d

14. trading   ____ a   ____ b   ____ c   ____ d

15. starring   ____ a   ____ b   ____ c   ____ d

WORD ANALYSIS   **A. 4. a.** Vowel in one-syllable word is short

DIRECTIONS: Say each word to yourself and listen to the vowel sound. Next to the word, write short if you hear a short vowel sound or long if you hear a long vowel sound.

1. ship _____

2. see _____

3. frog _____

4. gold _____

5. bed _____

6. sell _____

7. bus _____

8. pass _____

9. feet _____

10. pen _____

11. met _____

12. dot _____

13. knee _____

14. cat _____

15. hen _____

A. DIRECTIONS: Write the words with short vowel sounds from the list below to fill in the blank spaces in the sentences.

ham	hat	top	dog	pond
nut	pet	pig	shop	hop

1. Mother bakes _____ for dinner on Saturday.

2. Tom wears a _____ on his head.

3. The squirrel could not find a _____ in the yard.

4. Peter has a _____ rabbit.

5. The jar was full of cookies and we could not put the _____ on it.

6. The baby _____ was very fat and pink.

7. Tom's _____ is called Snoopy.

8. Susan went to the _____ to see the turtle.

9. The girls bought chocolates at the candy _____.

10. The rabbit likes to _____.

B. DIRECTIONS: Using the letters a, e, i, o, and u, make words with short vowel sounds. Each letter may be used more than once.

1. g __ s	5. r __ n	9. sh __ ll
2. l __ ck	6. c __ lf	10. t __ n
3. m __ p	7. b __ n	11. st __ p
4. fr __ g	8. sl __ d	12. b __ g

WORD ANALYSIS   **A.   4. b.** Vowel in syllable or word ending in *e* is long

DIRECTIONS: Say the words to yourself and listen to the vowel sounds. If the vowel sound is short, write <u>short</u> next to the word; if the vowel sound is long, write <u>long</u> next to the word.

1. fix	_____	11. tape	_____
2. cake	_____	12. face	_____
3. tub	_____	13. bee	_____
4. code	_____	14. tent	_____
5. dish	_____	15. date	_____
6. fine	_____	16. clap	_____
7. shape	_____	17. nose	_____
8. park	_____	18. dress	_____
9. size	_____	19. five	_____
10. bite	_____	20. dive	_____

WORD ANALYSIS   A. 4. b. Vowel in syllable or word ending in *e* is long

DIRECTIONS: Use the words at the top of each section to complete the sentences. Be sure to use a long vowel word.

dim	hid	cap	take
dime	hides	bake	cape

1. Sue paid a _____ for the candy.

2. The baby _____ from Mother.

3. Mother will _____ a chocolate cake.

4. Superman's _____ was caught in a phone booth.

5. Dad will _____ us to the circus.

rake	cake	gate	white
wipe	wip	cak	rak

6. Peggy will _____ the leaves.

7. Tom ate his birthday _____ .

8. The _____ swung open when the wind blew.

9. The _____ dress looked nice on Betty.

10. Mother said, " _____ your feet before you come in."

tame	late	bike	June
tune	Jun	lat	bik

11. The _____ lion did not roar or snarl.

12. They hurried so they would not be _____ for the party.

13. Tim's _____ is blue.

14. The school year ends in _____ .

15. He played a nice _____ on his flute.

WORD ANALYSIS   A.   4.   **a.** Vowel in one-syllable word is short
                                   b. Vowel in syllable or word ending in *e* is long

DIRECTIONS: Read the words below. If the vowel in the word is long, print <u>L</u> on the line. If the vowel in the word is short, print <u>S</u> on the line.

1. lad	_____	13. six	_____	25. man	_____
2. rope	_____	14. cute	_____	26. hole	_____
3. tug	_____	15. fun	_____	27. name	_____
4. mule	_____	16. kite	_____	28. cube	_____
5. hope	_____	17. pick	_____	29. swim	_____
6. tack	_____	18. deck	_____	30. nose	_____
7. hum	_____	19. stop	_____	31. lame	_____
8. slip	_____	20. bone	_____	32. pipe	_____
9. fan	_____	21. lick	_____	33. rob	_____
10. joke	_____	22. time	_____	34. zone	_____
11. lake	_____	23. cane	_____	35. note	_____
12. plan	_____	24. pill	_____	36. tube	_____

WORD ANALYSIS   A. 4. c. Two vowels together, first is often long and second is silent

DIRECTIONS: Fill in the missing long vowel sound word in each sentence.

1. Marguerite likes cherry _____.   pie, tie, lie

2. John will _____ the gate.   paint, faint, train

3. Do not lose my _____.   coat, tote, coal

4. The frogs _____ at night.   croak, coat, goat

5. Jim's dog likes to eat _____.   met, meat, make

6. Sue has a _____ bike.   cream, crime, green

7. Dad got a _____ for Christmas.   lie, die, tie

8. The name of the _____ is Bluefish.   boat, coat, float

9. Mother reminded us to use _____   soap, seek, soak
   when we take our baths.

10. The _____ car was in a wreck.   blew, blue, blow

11. The raft will _____ to shore.   flood, float, floor

12. The man's _____ were frozen.   feet, fell, felt

13. Green _____ are good to eat.   peas, pay, paw

14. The _____ ate the wash that was   goat, coat, tote
    on the line.

15. The _____ played with balls every   sea, see, seals
    day at five.

WORD ANALYSIS   **A.   4.   c.** Two vowels together, first is often long and second is silent

DIRECTIONS: When two vowels are together, the first is often long and the second is silent. Read each word. If the word does not fit the rule, draw a line through it.

1. roof	16. stool
2. sheep	17. sleep
3. boat	18. tooth
4. pause	19. beads
5. tea	20. sauce
6. bread	21. meat
7. coat	22. bean
8. sneeze	23. ray
9. peach	24. nail
10. float	25. roar
11. head	26. shoot
12. gray	27. stain
13. leaf	28. knee
14. haul	29. air
15. street	30. snail

Name: _____ Date: _____

A. DIRECTIONS: In the following words, underline the long vowels and draw a circle around the silent vowels.

1. r e a d		9. c o a s t
2. s a y		10. w h o a
3. w e a k		11. m e a t
4. w h e a t		12. f e a s t
5. t e a m		13. b e e f
6. d a y		14. s t e a m
7. s n a i l		15. b e a k
8. n a i l		

B. DIRECTIONS: Match a word in the first column with a word that has the same sound in the second column. Draw a line from the first word to the second word.

1. beam		a. float
2. hay		b. stead
3. peace		c. creep
4. roam		d. fleece
5. thread		e. cream
6. neat		f. toy
7. leap		g. foam
8. joy		h. seed
9. coat		i. seat
10. weed		j. lay

III

WORD ANALYSIS   **A. 4. d.** Vowel alone in word is short

DIRECTIONS: A vowel alone in a word is usually short. Say each of these words and listen to the vowel sound. If the word follows this rule, write <u>Yes</u>. If the word does not follow the rule, write <u>No</u>.

1. oh _____	11. two _____
2. limb _____	12. wild _____
3. go _____	13. old _____
4. stall _____	14. glow _____
5. berth _____	15. sigh _____
6. hi _____	16. bolt _____
7. blind _____	17. wash _____
8. ball _____	18. cloth _____
9. be _____	19. sign _____
10. both _____	20. tell _____

WORD ANALYSIS   **A.   4. d.** Vowel alone in word is short

DIRECTIONS: A vowel alone in a word is usually short. Say each of these words and listen to the vowel sound. If the word has a long vowel sound, write <u>long</u> on the line next to the word. If the word has a short vowel sound, write <u>short</u> on the line next to the word.

1. red _____   14. find _____

2. drink _____   15. well _____

3. be _____   16. with _____

4. got _____   17. wash _____

5. call _____   18. day _____

6. he _____   19. ran _____

7. cut _____   20. I _____

8. did _____   21. so _____

9. this _____   22. me _____

10. who _____   23. bow _____

11. hot _____   24. won _____

12. fast _____   25. tap _____

13. hop _____

Name: _____ Date: _____

WORD ANALYSIS   A. 4. a,b,c,d. Review of vowel rules

DIRECTIONS: Write on the line next to each word whether the vowel sound is short or long. Then, mark the letter or letters of the alphabet that tell which vowel rule applies to that word.

a. Vowel in one-syllable word is short.
b. Vowel in syllable or word ending in e is long.
c. Two vowels together, first is often long and second is silent.
d. Vowel alone in word is short.

1. lame _____ __ a __ b __ c __ d
2. ham _____ __ a __ b __ c __ d
3. block _____ __ a __ b __ c __ d
4. rose _____ __ a __ b __ c __ d
5. pen _____ __ a __ b __ c __ d
6. wine _____ __ a __ b __ c __ d
7. plan _____ __ a __ b __ c __ d
8. bit _____ __ a __ b __ c __ d
9. at _____ __ a __ b __ c __ d
10. tub _____ __ a __ b __ c __ d
11. hate _____ __ a __ b __ c __ d
12. rock _____ __ a __ b __ c __ d
13. bake _____ __ a __ b __ c __ d
14. sleep _____ __ a __ b __ c __ d
15. cot _____ __ a __ b __ c __ d

WORD ANALYSIS   **A.   4. a,b,c,d.** Review of vowel rules

DIRECTIONS: Write the word that best fits the sentence on the blank line.

1. I _____ Grandpa will come.   hop   hope

2. You may _____ my pencil.   us   use

3. Do you have a _____ ?   dim   dime

4. She needs a _____ for her dress.   pin   pine

5. Sam took a _____ out of the apple.   bit   bite

6. Jim is _____ school.   at   ate

7. Mother _____ the cake.   cut   cute

8. George wears a yellow _____ .   hat   hate

9. Bob has a new fishing _____ .   rod   rode

10. Peggy sent a _____ to her mother.   not   note

11. The red _____ is for Nyette.   box   boxe

12. The new _____ is for Jack.   bik   bike

13. June used a _____ to catch the fish.   net   neat

14. The _____ is old and rotten.   pal   pail

15. The dog _____ the large bone.   hid   hide

16. The flowers were placed in the _____ .   vas   vase

17. The lion was not _____ .   tam   tame

18. Kathryn played a _____ on the piano.   tun   tune

19. I like chocolate _____ .   cak   cake

20. The _____ was open when we came.   gat   gate

WORD ANALYSIS   A. 4. a,b,c,d. Review of vowel rules

DIRECTIONS: Check which vowel sound you hear in the underlined word.

1. The lone gunman robbed the store.   ____long   ____short

2. Brave men fought the battle.   ____long   ____short

3. Greg hopes to be an artist.   ____long   ____short

4. The circus act was funny.   ____long   ____short

5. The rich man gave food to the poor.   ____long   ____short

6. The witch didn't have a single tooth.   ____long   ____short

7. Smith Street is now being paved.   ____long   ____short

8. Margo dreams of taking a trip.   ____long   ____short

9. The nurse treats the sick man kindly.   ____long   ____short

10. Is it true that he flew to the moon?   ____long   ____short

11. The stool is low and not very handy.   ____long   ____short

12. The man was weak and tired.   ____long   ____short

13. The tall giant was angry.   ____long   ____short

14. Tim listened to the wise old man.   ____long   ____short

15. Chris got mud on his new shirt.   ____long   ____short

16. The ship will sail at six today.   ____long   ____short

17. Louise cried as she read the sad story.   ____long   ____short

18. The deer ran swiftly.   ____long   ____short

19. Mother told us not to get our feet wet.   ____long   ____short

20. The king was a kind man.   ____long   ____short

WORD ANALYSIS   **A. 4. a,b,c,d.** Review of vowel rules

DIRECTIONS: Match the word in Column A with a word in Column B that has the same sound.

Part I: ## Part II:

Column A	Column B	Column A	Column B
1. gay	_____ a. tall	1. sheep	_____ a. smoke
2. pet	_____ b. nut	2. page	_____ b. rate
3. clock	_____ c. lay	3. grow	_____ c. beet
4. plan	_____ d. mope	4. bean	_____ d. blue
5. fall	_____ e. dish	5. coat	_____ e. lie
6. fish	_____ f. drip	6. five	_____ f. wage
7. hope	_____ g. trim	7. tie	_____ g. show
8. cut	_____ h. fan	8. true	_____ h. mean
9. pin	_____ i. let	9. stove	_____ i. dive
10. slip	_____ j. dock	10. hate	_____ j. float

WORD ANALYSIS   A. 4. a,b,c,d. Review of vowel rules

DIRECTIONS: Check which rule or rules tells what the vowel sound is in the underlined word in each sentence.

a. Vowel in one-syllable word is short.
b. Vowel in syllable or word ending in e is long.
c. Two vowels together, first is often long and second is silent.
d. Vowel alone in word is short.

1. The tight rope hurt the woman's arm.   __a __b __c __d

2. The white car won the race.   __a __b __c __d

3. The wolf was lean and angry.   __a __b __c __d

4. The women sipped their tea quietly.   __a __b __c __d

5. What size shirt do you wear?   __a __b __c __d

6. It is very hot today.   __a __b __c __d

7. The clock was very old but very pretty.   __a __b __c __d

8. The pitch was wild and off-base.   __a __b __c __d

9. The sign on the grass said "Keep Off."   __a __b __c __d

10. The road was muddy and slippery.   __a __b __c __d

11. The dog likes to chase the rabbit.   __a __b __c __d

12. Tom's chest hurt.   __a __b __c __d

13. Mice and men like cheese.   __a __b __c __d

14. Can your dog do tricks?   __a __b __c __d

15. The giant spoke loudly.   __a __b __c __d

WORD ANALYSIS   A. 5. C *followed by* i, e, y *makes s sound*
                            C *followed by* a, o, u *makes k sound*

DIRECTIONS: Write the following words under the correct headings.

When c is followed by i, e, or y, the c usually makes an s sound.
When c is followed by a, o, or u, the c usually makes a k sound.

come	city	Cuba
control	case	count
customer	center	coral
caught	cold	circle
cent	coin	cell

C = S Sound   C = K Sound

_____   _____

_____   _____

_____   _____

_____   _____

_____   _____

_____   _____

_____   _____

_____   _____

_____   _____

WORD ANALYSIS   A. 5. C *followed by* i, e, y *makes* s *sound*
C *followed by* a, o, u *makes* k *sound*

DIRECTIONS: Circle the correct beginning sound for each word. If the <u>c</u> has the <u>s</u> sound, circle the <u>S</u>; if the <u>c</u> has the <u>k</u> sound, circle the <u>K</u>.

		S	K
1.	cargo	S	K
2.	coat	S	K
3.	cement	S	K
4.	cabbage	S	K
5.	cite	S	K
6.	cattle	S	K
7.	circus	S	K
8.	cobra	S	K
9.	coconut	S	K
10.	cycle	S	K
11.	contract	S	K
12.	cost	S	K
13.	corn	S	K
14.	cypress	S	K
15.	camp	S	K
16.	cuticle	S	K
17.	candle	S	K
18.	civic	S	K
19.	cotton	S	K
20.	civil	S	K

WORD ANALYSIS   A. 5. C *followed by* i, e, y *makes* s *sound*
                          C *followed by* a, o, u *makes* k *sound*

DIRECTIONS: Read each sentence and circle the S if the c in the underlined word has an s sound, or circle the K if the c in the underlined word has a k sound.

S K   1. Tom wanted a camera for his birthday.

S K   2. The cable car puffed up the hill.

S K   3. The castle was built on the mountainside.

S K   4. My cousin lives in Texas.

S K   5. The computer disk whirled and whirled and finally stopped.

S K   6. The concert begins at eight.

S K   7. The Indians captured the young boy.

S K   8. The mat read "Welcome."

S K   9. Tom received a letter and a postcard.

S K 10. Red carnations are my favorite flower.

S K 11. The weather forecast is for rain and sleet.

S K 12. Since the first of September, Jill has been absent five days.

S K 13. The farmer grew a lot of cotton and soybeans.

S K 14. That large piece of pie is for Jack.

S K 15. Betty likes coconut cake.

S K 16. The telephone caller was polite.

S K 17. Boiled cabbage is a delicious dish.

S K 18. The judge entered the courthouse.

S K 19. Dad has had a bad cold for days.

S K 20. The castle door was locked.

WORD ANALYSIS   **A.** **5.** **C** *followed by* i, e, y *makes* s *sound*
                            C *followed by* a, o, u *makes* k *sound*

DIRECTIONS: Print <u>S</u> if the word has a soft <u>c</u> sound; print <u>K</u> if the word has a hard <u>c</u> sound.

_____	1. nice	_____	11. curl
_____	2. second	_____	12. comma
_____	3. fence	_____	13. France
_____	4. ice	_____	14. cookie
_____	5. coil	_____	15. current
_____	6. space	_____	16. captain
_____	7. ocean	_____	17. twice
_____	8. cottage	_____	18. force
_____	9. chance	_____	19. comfort
_____	10. capital	_____	20. cork

WORD ANALYSIS   A. 5. C *followed by* i, e, y *makes s sound*
C *followed by* a, o, u *makes k sound*

DIRECTIONS: Classify the following into words with a c that makes an s sound and words with a c that makes a k sound.

concrete	canyon	code	face
acid	Africa	circle	glance
juice	carve	cake	suitcase
acorn	cave	special	voice
contract	pencil	place	because
cover	decide	fence	cymbal

C = S Sound   C = K Sound

_____   _____

_____   _____

_____   _____

_____   _____

_____   _____

_____   _____

_____   _____

_____   _____

_____   _____

_____   _____

_____   _____

_____   _____

WORD ANALYSIS   A.   6.   **G** *followed by* **i, e, y** *makes* **j** *sound*
                                  G *followed by* **a, o, u** *makes* **guh** *sound*

DIRECTIONS: When a g̲ is followed by i̲, e̲, or y̲, the g̲ usually makes a j sound. When a g̲ is followed by a̲, o̲, or u̲, the g̲ usually makes a guh̅ sound. Write the following words under the correct headings.

ginger   giraffe   guy
game   giant   good
goose   guitar   golden
got   gum   gem
gut   gym   gentle
generate   gate   gang

G = J Sound   G = Guh Sound

_____   _____

_____   _____

_____   _____

_____   _____

_____   _____

_____   _____

_____   _____

_____   _____

_____   _____

_____   _____

WORD ANALYSIS   A. 6. G *followed by* i, e, y *makes* j *sound*
                         G *followed by* a, o, u *makes* guh *sound*

DIRECTIONS: Circle the correct beginning sound for each word. If the g has the j (soft) sound, circle the j; if the g has the guh (hard) sound, circle the guh.

1. guitar	j	guh
2. garden	j	guh
3. go	j	guh
4. gun	j	guh
5. garage	j	guh
6. giraffe	j	guh
7. goat	j	guh
8. get	j	guh
9. germ	j	guh
10. guess	j	guh
11. guinea	j	guh
12. gin	j	guh
13. gem	j	guh
14. goes	j	guh
15. gentleness	j	guh
16. gold	j	guh
17. gee	j	guh
18. gene	j	guh
19. gumbo	j	guh
20. gypsy	j	guh

WORD ANALYSIS   A. 6. G *followed by* i, e, y *makes* j *sound*
                       G *followed by* a, o, u *makes* guh *sound*

DIRECTIONS: Read the sentence and circle the j if the g has a soft sound or circle the guh if the g has a hard sound.

j guh 1. The <u>alligator</u> lay in the warm sun for hours.

j guh 2. At what <u>age</u> did she win the gold medal?

j guh 3. The Indian walked <u>against</u> the windblown snow.

j guh 4. The race <u>began</u> at seven in the morning.

j guh 5. The fairy broke the <u>magic</u> spell.

j guh 6. The pudding was <u>good</u>.

j guh 7. The boy was scared and sat on the <u>edge</u> of his chair.

j guh 8. The homework is on <u>page</u> 47.

j guh 9. The <u>wagon</u> train master was tall and lean.

j guh 10. The <u>goalkeeper</u> caught the puck.

j guh 11. <u>August</u> is the eighth month of the year.

j guh 12. The sea <u>voyage</u> lasted thirty days.

j guh 13. The <u>governor</u> was inaugurated on the sixth of January.

j guh 14. The house had four <u>regular</u> ghosts and two visiting ghosts.

j guh 15. A cold is caused by a <u>germ</u>.

WORD ANALYSIS   A. 6. G *followed by* i, e, y *makes* j *sound*
                                G *followed by* a, o, u *makes* guh *sound*

DIRECTIONS: Print j if the word has a soft g sound; print guh if the word has a hard g sound.

_____	1. engine	_____	11. orange
_____	2. huge	_____	12. large
_____	3. Roger	_____	13. gaze
_____	4. original	_____	14. fringe
_____	5. gay	_____	15. change
_____	6. gulp	_____	16. gabby
_____	7. damage	_____	17. gather
_____	8. gallop	_____	18. refrigerator
_____	9. galoshes	_____	19. hangar
_____	10. strange	_____	20. cottage

WORD ANALYSIS   A.   6. G *followed by* i, e, y *makes* j *sound*
                            G *followed by* a, o, u *makes* guh *sound*

DIRECTIONS: Classify the following into words with a soft g sound (j) and words with a hard g sound (guh).

goblin	gutter
wedge	voyage
argument	urge
bulge	judge
elegant	cargo
engine	hogan
mango	gable
general	genius
serge	gust
goal	guess

G = Soft Sound = J   G = Hard Sound = Guh

_____   _____

_____   _____

_____   _____

_____   _____

_____   _____

_____   _____

_____   _____

_____   _____

_____   _____

_____   _____

WORD ANALYSIS   A.   7. *Silent letters in* kn, wr, gn

DIRECTIONS: Circle the silent consonant in each word.

1. write	11. gnu
2. wrap	12. gnat
3. knot	13. knee
4. gnaw	14. wrote
5. wrong	15. know
6. gnarl	16. wring
7. knock	17. gnome
8. wreak	18. knife
9. kneel	19. wrong
10. gnash	20. knight

WORD ANALYSIS   A. 7. *Silent letters in* kn, wr, gn

DIRECTIONS: Read the sentences. When you come to a word that has a part missing, write in a consonant cluster to make the right word.

kn   wr   gn

1. Grandma likes to _____ it.

2. _____ ing out your wet towel.

3. Wood with a _____ arl is hard to cut.

4. Peggy fell and scraped her _____ ee.

5. Gary hurt his _____ ist and cannot play ball.

6. The new book on _____ omes is in the library.

7. The scouts learned how to tie _____ ots.

8. The giant _____ ashed his teeth and groaned.

9. The _____ ife was very sharp.

10. The clothes came out of the dryer without a _____ inkle.

11. A _____ u is an African antelope.

12. Sam likes to _____ ite letters.

13. A _____ at bit Alex on his hand.

14. The lion _____ awed on the bone.

15. Jacob gave the _____ ong answer on his test.

16. _____ ock on the door before you enter.

WORD ANALYSIS   A. 7. *Silent letters in* kn, wr, gn

A. DIRECTIONS: Write a <u>kn</u> word that rhymes with each of the following.

snow	1. _____	fit	6. _____
rock	2. _____	flew	7. _____
shot	3. _____	fell	8. _____
rob	4. _____	sack	9. _____
roll	5. _____	read	10. _____

B. DIRECTIONS: Write a <u>wr</u> word that rhymes with each of the following.

nap	1. _____	neck	6. _____
sack	2. _____	pen	7. _____
sing	3. _____	long	8. _____
fist	4. _____	why	9. _____
path	5. _____	vote	10. _____

WORD ANALYSIS   A.   7. *Silent letters in* kn, wr, gn

DIRECTIONS: Select the word that best completes the sentence and write the word on the blank line.

1. The man was told to _____ three times on the green door.
      knock   rock

2. The airplane _____ was towed away.
      deck   wreck

3. The old woman's hands were _____.
      gnarled   snarled

4. The _____ on the door would not turn.
        pane   knob

5. The football player broke his _____.
      knee   free

6. The _____ was long and sharp.
        rife   knife

7. The stranger could not undo the _____.
      knot   lot

8. The lady put on her _____ and left the party.
      slap   wrap

9. A _____ is a little brown bird.
      wren   glen

10. Marie sprained her _____ playing ball.
      wrist   twist

11. The _____ truck came to the scene of the accident.
        decker   wrecker

12. The Christmas _____ was hung on the door.
      breath   wreath

13. The _____ came out at night and danced with the flowers.
        gnome   home

14. There was a swarm of _____ in the swamp.
      gnats   cats

15. Mother will _____ me a sweater.
        fret   knit

WORD ANALYSIS   A.   7. *Silent letters in* kn, wr, gn

DIRECTIONS: Circle the silent consonant in each word.

1. gnashing

2. wrangle

3. writer

4. knight

5. wrestling

6. wristlet

7. knickers

8. wrench

9. knelt

10. wringer

11. wreckage

12. gnawing

13. kneepad

14. gnomes

15. knotted

16. wrapper

17. knitting

18. gnat

19. knapsack

20. wrongly

A. DIRECTIONS: Write the plural of each of the following words.

1. puppy	_____	6. tunnel	_____
2. glove	_____	7. bottle	_____
3. tax	_____	8. twenty	_____
4. knife	_____	9. kiss	_____
5. pretzel	_____	10. half	_____

B. DIRECTIONS: The following words are plurals. Write the singular form of each one.

1. calves	_____	6. bullets	_____
2. mongooses	_____	7. funnies	_____
3. guests	_____	8. ranches	_____
4. harnesses	_____	9. sandwiches	_____
5. scarves	_____	10. bunnies	_____

WORD ANALYSIS   B. 1. *Forming plurals*

DIRECTIONS: Match the plural form of the word with the singular form.

Part A.

1. lake   —   a. groceries

2. mess   —   b. glasses

3. grocery   —   c. messages

4. turnip   —   d. shelves

5. ash   —   e. wives

6. jelly   —   f. lakes

7. glass   —   g. messes

8. wife   —   h. ashes

9. shelf   —   i. jellies

10. message   —   j. turnips

Part B.

1. bricks   —   a. story

2. pennies   —   b. ring

3. rings   —   c. faucet

4. thieves   —   d. penny

5. eggs   —   e. leaf

6. stories   —   f. thief

7. leaves   —   g. egg

8. bodies   —   h. brick

9. faucets   —   i. dress

10. dresses   —   j. body

WORD ANALYSIS   B. 1. *Forming plurals*

DIRECTIONS: You are given the singular form of a word in the column on the left. Select the correct plural spelling of the word from the choices on the right.

1. sheaf   ____ a. sheafes   ____ b. sheaves   ____ c. sheafs

2. den   ____ a. dens   ____ b. denes   ____ c. denies

3. family   ____ a. familys   ____ b. familyies   ____ c. families

4. flipper   ____ a. flippers   ____ b. flipperes   ____ c. flipperies

5. flag   ____ a. flagies   ____ b. flags   ____ c. flaves

6. circus   ____ a. circus   ____ b. circuses   ____ c. circusies

7. loaf   ____ a. loafs   ____ b. loafies   ____ c. loaves

8. day   ____ a. days   ____ b. daies   ____ c. dayes

9. closet   ____ a. closets   ____ b. closetes   ____ c. closeties

10. branch   ____ a. branchies   ____ b. branches   ____ c. branchs

11. tadpole   ____ a. tadpoleies   ____ b. tadpoles   ____ c. tadpole

12. elf   ____ a. elves   ____ b. elfs   ____ c. elfies

13. daisy   ____ a. daisies   ____ b. daisyes   ____ c. daisyies

14. lunch   ____ a. lunchies   ____ b. lunches   ____ c. lunchs

15. wolf   ____ a. wolves   ____ b. wolfes   ____ c. wolies

III

WORD ANALYSIS   B. 1. *Forming plurals*

DIRECTIONS: Write the plural of each of these words.

1. duck   _____

2. baby   _____

3. ranch   _____

4. wolf   _____

5. rag   _____

6. class   _____

7. bowl   _____

8. self   _____

9. sky   _____

10. lass   _____

11. calf   _____

12. farm   _____

13. fly   _____

14. inch   _____

15. bridge   _____

16. bat   _____

17. country   _____

18. raccoon   _____

19. loaf   _____

20. lady   _____

Name: _____ Date: _____

WORD ANALYSIS   B. 1. *Forming plurals*

DIRECTIONS: You are given the plural form of a word in the column on the left. Select the correct singular spelling of the word from the choices on the right.

1. letters ____ a. lette ____ b. letter ____ c. letters

2. halves ____ a. halv ____ b. half ____ c. halve

3. foxes ____ a. foxe ____ b. fox ____ c. foxes

4. batches ____ a. batch ____ b. batc ____ c. batche

5. stations ____ a. statio ____ b. station ____ c. stat

6. diaries ____ a. diary ____ b. diarie ____ c. diari

7. skates ____ a. skat ____ b. skate ____ c. ska

8. punches ____ a. punch ____ b. punc ____ c. punche

9. shelves ____ a. shelv ____ b. shelve ____ c. shelf

10. lorries ____ a. lorrie ____ b. lorri ____ c. lorry

11. watches ____ a. watch ____ b. watche ____ c. watc

12. cities ____ a. citie ____ b. citi ____ c. city

13. goats ____ a. goat ____ b. goa ____ c. goats

14. guesses ____ a. guesse ____ b. guess ____ c. gues

15. whistles ____ a. whistl ____ b. whist ____ c. whistle

WORD ANALYSIS   B. 2. *Similarities of sound*

DIRECTIONS: Tell what sound is heard in the underlined letters.

1. c̲at   _____

2. lau̲n̲dry   _____

3. cou̲g̲h   _____

4. raspberr̲y̲   _____

5. f̲un   _____

6. k̲iss   _____

7. c̲upboard   _____

8. telep̲hone   _____

9. gas̲k̲et   _____

10. nat̲i̲o̲n   _____

11. ac̲h̲e   _____

12. priso̲n̲   _____

13. snac̲k̲   _____

14. joll̲y̲   _____

15. jugg̲l̲e   _____

DIRECTIONS: For each word in the first column, find the word in the second column where the underlined letters make the same sound. Write the letter in the blank.

Part A.

___ 1. knock   a. staff

___ 2. fox   b. oar

___ 3. tux   c. ducks

___ 4. bowl   d. nod

___ 5. noose   e. locks

___ 6. blouse   f. foal

___ 7. snore   g. introduce

___ 8. graph   h. plows

Part B.

___ 1. four   a. moose

___ 2. juice   b. goes

___ 3. gloom   c. score

___ 4. spruce   d. break

___ 5. blew   e. deuce

___ 6. glows   f. bound

___ 7. wake   g. blue

___ 8. town   h. plume

WORD ANALYSIS **B. 2.** *Similarities of sound*

DIRECTIONS: For each word at the beginning of the line, circle a word to
the right where the underlined letters make the same sound.

1. ch<u>ew</u>	a. beg<u>e</u>t	b. y<u>ou</u>	c. fr<u>e</u>t
2. p<u>ou</u>nd	a. c<u>o</u>ne	b. p<u>o</u>nd	c. fr<u>ow</u>n
3. b<u>ow</u>	a. b<u>ou</u>gh	b. <u>w</u>omen	c. m<u>o</u>re
4. m<u>ee</u>k	a. str<u>ea</u>k	b. l<u>e</u>ft	c. m<u>e</u>t
5. cr<u>ow</u>n	a. cr<u>ow</u>	b. gr<u>ou</u>nd	c. str<u>aw</u>
6. res<u>ume</u>	a. r<u>oo</u>m	b. m<u>um</u>	c. f<u>un</u>
7. gr<u>ea</u>t	a. b<u>ee</u>t	b. c<u>a</u>ke	c. s<u>ee</u>
8. thr<u>ew</u>	a. y<u>ou</u>	b. g<u>o</u>	c. fl<u>ow</u>
9. d<u>u</u>ke	a. mus<u>i</u>c	b. <u>k</u>it	c. sp<u>oo</u>k
10. can<u>oe</u>	a. fl<u>ow</u>	b. kn<u>ew</u>	c. <u>o</u>boe
11. s<u>ue</u>	a. sh<u>ow</u>	b. m<u>ow</u>	c. scr<u>ew</u>
12. so<u>ck</u>s	a. bo<u>x</u>	b. yel<u>low</u>	c. bro<u>wn</u>
13. tr<u>e</u>k	a. b<u>a</u>ck	b. wr<u>e</u>ck	c. <u>a</u>ge
14. cr<u>ee</u>k	a. p<u>ea</u>k	b. m<u>a</u>ke	c. s<u>i</u>nk
15. c<u>o</u>de	a. <u>a</u>dd	b. bas<u>e</u>	c. l<u>oa</u>d

WORD ANALYSIS   B.   2. *Similarities of sound*

DIRECTIONS: For each word in the first column, find the word in the second column where the underlined letters make the same sound. Write the letter in the blank.

Part A.   ___ 1. br<u>ow</u>n   a. w<u>ou</u>ld

        ___ 2. w<u>oo</u>d   b. br<u>aw</u>l

        ___ 3. s<u>o</u>   c. ar<u>ou</u>nd

        ___ 4. p<u>oo</u>l   d. b<u>ack</u>s

        ___ 5. w<u>ax</u>   e. sh<u>ower</u>s

        ___ 6. ph<u>one</u>   f. fl<u>ow</u>

        ___ 7. b<u>all</u>   g. r<u>u</u>le

        ___ 8. <u>our</u>s   h. l<u>oa</u>n

Part B.   ___ 1. <u>li</u>nks   a. t<u>oa</u>d

        ___ 2. w<u>orm</u>   b. r<u>oo</u>t

        ___ 3. r<u>ode</u>   c. wr<u>ote</u>

        ___ 4. br<u>oke</u>   d. t<u>erm</u>

        ___ 5. ch<u>oose</u>   e. l<u>y</u>nx

        ___ 6. f<u>l</u>ute   f. sm<u>all</u>

        ___ 7. fl<u>oa</u>t   g. cr<u>oa</u>k

        ___ 8. m<u>au</u>l   h. cr<u>uise</u>

WORD ANALYSIS   B.   2. *Similarities of sound*

A. DIRECTIONS: Match the sound of the underlined part of the word in the first column with a sound in the second column.

____	1. gnaw	a.	ôl
____	2. clay	b.	n
____	3. baggy	c.	kr
____	4. all	d.	r
____	5. grocer	e.	kwes
____	6. crow	f.	k
____	7. wren	g.	ē
____	8. question	h.	ser

B. DIRECTIONS: Match the word in the first column with a word in the second column where the underlined letters make the same sound.

____	1. crown	a.	graph
____	2. half	b.	ox
____	3. knot	c.	kraft
____	4. gale	d.	hours
____	5. troop	e.	note
____	6. clocks	f.	boys
____	7. flowers	g.	frail
____	8. poise	h.	soup

A. DIRECTIONS: Write the Arabic numerals for the following Roman numerals.

a. I _____		f. V _____	
b. IV _____		g. III _____	
c. VI _____		h. IX _____	
d. II _____		i. VIII _____	
e. X _____		j. VII _____	

B. DIRECTIONS: Write the Roman numerals for the following Arabic numerals.

a. 10 _____		f. 2 _____	
b. 6 _____		g. 9 _____	
c. 3 _____		h. 4 _____	
d. 1 _____		i. 7 _____	
e. 8 _____		j. 5 _____	

WORD ANALYSIS   **B. 3.** *Roman numerals* **I** *through* **X**

DIRECTIONS: In each sentence, write a Roman numeral for the underlined word.

1. The pig had <u>three</u> (_____) eyes.

2. The <u>ten</u> (_____) legs of the monster were very different.

3. <u>Five</u> (_____) cents is a nickel.

4. <u>One</u> (_____) piece of gum was mine.

5. A pair of something is <u>two</u> (_____).

6. <u>Nine</u> (_____) girls went to the ball game.

7. The circus had <u>eight</u> (_____) clowns.

8. <u>Four</u> (_____) lions were ill.

9. The <u>six</u> (_____) elephants paraded under the big top.

10. The trainer worked with <u>seven</u> (_____) lions at one time.

11. Only <u>one</u> (_____) clown looked sad.

12. The monkey ate <u>five</u> (_____) bananas.

13. The elephant needed <u>ten</u> (_____) buckets of water.

14. <u>Five</u> (_____) bears were brown.

15. I only saw <u>one</u> (_____) giraffe.

WORD ANALYSIS   B.   3. *Roman numerals* I *through* X

DIRECTIONS: At the end of each sentence, write the Arabic numeral for the Roman numeral in the sentence.

1. The horse won VIII races. _____

2. Tom rode Horse III. _____

3. Kathryn's horse took the number II spot. _____

4. The V horses were brown and white. _____

5. Gary's father fed X horses grain. _____

6. Only IX horses need to be watered. _____

7. There was room in the barn for VII horses. _____

8. VI boys cleaned the stalls. _____

9. The stalls needed IV bales of hay. _____

10. The horses were kept in Barn I. _____

11. Quick Silver won on day X. _____

12. He just wants to win I race. _____

13. Carlos won V races on Tuesday. _____

14. Kim will race her horse on March V. _____

15. Amy won the race on April I. _____

Name: _____ Date: _____

WORD ANALYSIS   B. 3. *Roman numerals* I *through* X

DIRECTIONS: Draw a circle around the Arabic numeral for the Roman numeral at the beginning of each line.

a. II   3   2   4

b. VI   6   4   7

c. X   1   5   10

d. IV   7   6   4

e. I   2   1   10

f. V   10   5   1

g. III   3   6   8

h. VII   8   7   9

i. X   1   5   10

j. V   5   10   1

k. I   10   1   5

l. VIII   3   9   8

m. X   10   5   1

n. IX   7   9   6

o. V   5   7   4

WORD ANALYSIS   B. 3. *Roman numerals* **I** *through* **X**

A. DIRECTIONS: Write the matching Roman numeral near the Arabic numeral.

a. 1 ____ VII   f. 10 ____ VIII

b. 7 ____ IV   g. 2 ____ IX

c. 3 ____ I   h. 9 ____ II

d. 4 ____ V   i. 6 ____ X

e. 5 ____ III   j. 8 ____ VI

B. DIRECTIONS: Write the Roman numeral for the underlined number in each sentence.

1. Sam had five (_____) sisters.

2. Two (_____) sisters had blue eyes.

3. One (_____) sister had green eyes.

4. Ten (_____) boys chased Sam after he teased them.

5. Each girl had five (_____) dolls.

6. One (_____) doll was broken.

7. It took ten (_____) days to mend the doll.

8. The five (_____) girls were very tall.

9. The girls had only one (_____) brother.

10. Ten (_____) eyes watched Sam all the time.

WORD ANALYSIS   C.   1. *As many syllables in a word as there are vowels*

DIRECTIONS: Write the number of syllables in each word on the line next to the word.

1. ants	_____		11. ladder	_____
2. husband	_____		12. pill	_____
3. now	_____		13. nest	_____
4. barber	_____		14. odor	_____
5. knapsack	_____		15. both	_____
6. Carol	_____		16. wig	_____
7. master	_____		17. zigzag	_____
8. lost	_____		18. hiccup	_____
9. speck	_____		19. slim	_____
10. net	_____		20. carrot	_____

DIRECTIONS: Circle the number of syllables in the word.

a.	spatter	1	2	3
b.	sniff	1	2	3
c.	turtle	1	2	3
d.	west	1	2	3
e.	thank	1	2	3
f.	storm	1	2	3
g.	bag	1	2	3
h.	almost	1	2	3
i.	find	1	2	3
j.	spun	1	2	3
k.	act	1	2	3
l.	fable	1	2	3
m.	butterfly	1	2	3
n.	bag	1	2	3
o.	alphabet	1	2	3
p.	rich	1	2	3
q.	title	1	2	3
r.	blackbird	1	2	3
s.	six	1	2	3
t.	purple	1	2	3

WORD ANALYSIS   C. 1. *As many syllables in a word as there are vowels*

DIRECTIONS: Listen for the syllables in each word and write the number of syllables on the line after the word.

Part A.

a. whether _____		k. himself _____
b. burn _____		l. rewarded _____
c. depend _____		m. collected _____
d. shallow _____		n. upright _____
e. scent _____		o. watermelon _____
f. scamper _____		p. sunlight _____
g. skidded _____		q. stoplight _____
h. whisper _____		r. spot _____
i. wedding _____		s. depended _____
j. walnut _____		t. stepmother _____

Part B.

a. admit _____		k. women _____
b. junk _____		l. window _____
c. yum _____		m. hopscotch _____
d. wonderful _____		n. follow _____
e. hospital _____		o. castle _____
f. if _____		p. bring _____
g. garden _____		q. barn _____
h. glad _____		r. along _____
i. fossil _____		s. winter _____
j. flip _____		t. antler _____

Name: _____ **Date:** _____

DIRECTIONS: Say each word. Listen to the number of vowel sounds in the word. Write the number of syllables in the space after each word.

1. tomorrow ____	16. pudding ____
2. perfect ____	17. bullet ____
3. umbrella ____	18. sandwich ____
4. cloth ____	19. pedal ____
5. Alaska ____	20. robot ____
6. reward ____	21. control ____
7. payment ____	22. surrender ____
8. won ____	23. flew ____
9. coral ____	24. cotton ____
10. sew ____	25. person ____
11. moment ____	26. buffalo ____
12. desert ____	27. mat ____
13. Pinta ____	28. hotel ____
14. volcano ____	29. puddle ____
15. December ____	30. thorn ____

WORD ANALYSIS   C.   1. *As many syllables in a word as there are vowels*

DIRECTIONS: Say the word and circle the number of syllables you hear.

a.	bicycle	1	2	3
b.	front	1	2	3
c.	higher	1	2	3
d.	can	1	2	3
e.	barber	1	2	3
f.	danger	1	2	3
g.	slowly	1	2	3
h.	open	1	2	3
i.	uncle	1	2	3
j.	mud	1	2	3
k.	hungry	1	2	3
l.	cowboy	1	2	3
m.	arrow	1	2	3
n.	spirit	1	2	3
o.	ladder	1	2	3
p.	burro	1	2	3
q.	better	1	2	3
r.	department	1	2	3
s.	computer	1	2	3
t.	chipmunk	1	2	3

WORD ANALYSIS   C. 2. *Single consonant between two vowels*

DIRECTIONS: Say the word to yourself. Write the word on the line and divide it into syllables.

1. seven _____

2. shovel _____

3. mesa _____

4. navel _____

5. closet _____

6. return _____

7. moment _____

8. coral _____

9. title _____

10. Nina _____

11. tuna _____

12. visit _____

13. hogan _____

14. second _____

15. paper _____

16. magic _____

17. locate _____

18. Lola _____

19. later _____

20. famous _____

WORD ANALYSIS   **C. 2.** *Single consonant between two vowels*

DIRECTIONS: Say the word. Place a check mark (✓) next to the word that is divided into syllables correctly.

1. forest ___ a. for / est ___ b. fo / rest ___ c. fore / st

2. tulip ___ a. tu / lip ___ b. tul / ip ___ c. tulip

3. clover ___ a. clov / er ___ b. clove/r ___ c. clo / ver

4. minus ___ a. minu / s ___ b. min / us ___ c. mi / nus

5. gravy ___ a. gravy ___ b. gra / vy ___ c. grav / y

6. wagon ___ a. wa / gon ___ b. wag / on ___ c. wago / n

7. vapor ___ a. vapor ___ b. vap / or ___ c. va / por

8. motion ___ a. moti / on ___ b. mo / tion ___ c. motio / n

9. beside ___ a. bes / ide ___ b. be / side ___ c. besi / de

10. cabin ___ a. ca / bin ___ b. cab / in ___ c. cabi / n

11. dragon ___ a. dr / agon ___ b. dra / gon ___ c. drag / on

12. favor ___ a. fa / vor ___ b. fav / or ___ c. favo / r

13. Judy ___ a. Judy ___ b. Jud / y ___ c. Ju / dy

14. mama ___ a. mam / a ___ b. ma / ma ___ c. mama

15. protect ___ a. pro / tect ___ b. prot / ect ___ c. pr / otect

WORD ANALYSIS   C. 2. *Single consonant between two vowels*

DIRECTIONS: Say the word to yourself and listen carefully. Write the word divided into syllables in the blank.

1. motor   _____

2. pretend   _____

3. about   _____

4. favor   _____

5. hotel   _____

6. radar   _____

7. ahead   _____

8. cable   _____

9. hero   _____

10. liter   _____

11. tiger   _____

12. noble   _____

13. salad   _____

14. locust   _____

15. behind   _____

16. mason   _____

17. peso   _____

18. clover   _____

19. salute   _____

20. stupid   _____

WORD ANALYSIS   **C.   2. *Single consonant between two vowels***

DIRECTIONS: Place a check mark (✓) on the line in front of the correct division of the word into syllables.

1. woman   ____ a. wom / an   ____ b. wo / man

2. nature   ____ a. na / ture   ____ b. nat / ure

3. lady   ____ a. la / dy   ____ b. lad / y

4. magic   ____ a. mag / ic   ____ b. ma / gic

5. open   ____ a. op / en   ____ b. o / pen

6. prefix   ____ a. pre / fix   ____ b. pref / ix

7. paper   ____ a. pa / per   ____ b. pap / er

8. present   ____ a. pre / sent   ____ b. pres / ent

9. belong   ____ a. bel / ong   ____ b. be / long

10. moment   ____ a. mo / ment   ____ b. mom / ent

11. travel   ____ a. trav / el   ____ b. tra / vel

12. spider   ____ a. spid / er   ____ b. spi / der

13. repay   ____ a. re / pay   ____ b. rep / ay

14. protect   ____ a. prot / ect   ____ b. pro / tect

15. decide   ____ a. de / cide   ____ b. dec / ide

16. notice   ____ a. no / tice   ____ b. not / ice

17. special   ____ a. spec / ial   ____ b. spe / cial

18. rotor   ____ a. ro / tor   ____ b. rot / or

19. plaza   ____ a. plaz / a   ____ b. pla / za

20. over   ____ a. ov / er   ____ b. o / ver

A. DIRECTIONS: Write each of the following words divided into syllables.

1. open _____   9. beaver _____

2. about _____   10. below _____

3. body _____   11. famous _____

4. lizard _____   12. idea _____

5. even _____   13. homer _____

6. finish _____   14. David _____

7. cozy _____   15. alike _____

8. closet _____

B. DIRECTIONS: Circle the correct division of each of the following words into syllables.

1. Lisa   a. Lis / a   b. Li / sa
2. labor   a. lab / or   b. la / bor
3. Eva   a. E / va   b. Ev / a
4. cement   a. ce / ment   b. cem / ent
5. saucer   a. sauc / er   b. sau / cer
6. hero   a. he / ro   b. her / o
7. awake   a. a / wake   b. aw / ake
8. obey   a. ob / ey   b. o / bey
9. tiny   a. ti / ny   b. tin / y
10. grocer   a. gro / cer   b. groc / er

DIRECTIONS: Write the following words divided into syllables.

1. battle   _____

2. nibble   _____

3. assure   _____

4. manner   _____

5. shudder   _____

6. little   _____

7. offer   _____

8. fellow   _____

9. robber   _____

10. lesson   _____

11. Roddy   _____

12. berry   _____

13. appear   _____

14. settle   _____

15. suggest   _____

WORD ANALYSIS   C. 3. *Double consonant*

DIRECTIONS: Circle the correct way to write each word divided into syllables.

1. bottle	a. bot / tle	b. bott / le
2. follow	a. fo / llow	b. fol / low
3. cattle	a. catt / le	b. cat / tle
4. sudden	a. sud / den	b. sudd / en
5. success	a. succ / ess	b. suc / cess
6. pepper	a. pep / per	b. pepp / er
7. worry	a. wor / ry	b. worr / y
8. killer	a. kille / r	b. kil / ler
9. pretty	a. pret / ty	b. prett / y
10. happy	a. ha / ppy	b. hap / py
11. hurry	a. hu / rry	b. hur / ry
12. funny	a. fun / ny	b. funn / y
13. allow	a. a / llow	b. al / low
14. nibble	a. nib / ble	b. ni / bble
15. letter	a. let / ter	b. le / tter
16. spatter	a. sp / atter	b. spat / ter
17. batter	a. ba / tter	b. bat / ter
18. puzzle	a. puz / zle	b. puzz / le
19. common	a. comm / on	b. com / mon
20. settle	a. set / tle	b. sett / le

WORD ANALYSIS   C. 3. *Double consonant*

DIRECTIONS: One word is missing in each of the following sentences. Choose one of the three words below the sentence to fill the blank by drawing a line under the word. Then draw lines between the syllables in all of the three words under the line.

1. The baby threw the _____ on the floor.
   rattle   cattle   little

2. The ball cost one _____ .
   pepper   dollar   letter

3. The pink dress has a white _____ .
   ruffle   manner   settle

4. The boy's name is _____ .
   Sammy   Nibble   Cattle

5. The cowboys were rounding up the _____ .
   common   cattle   batter

6. Joan likes to _____ dolls.
   collect   suppose   burrow

7. The clown carried twenty _____ .
   follow   spatter   balloons

8. Joan likes _____ on her sandwich.
   letter   lettuce   litter

9. The _____ broke into a hundred pieces.
   assure   middle   mirror

10. The hall was long and _____ .
    saddle   narrow   smelling

WORD ANALYSIS   C.   3. *Double consonant*

DIRECTIONS: Write each of the following words divided into syllables.

1. dribble   _____

2. puppy   _____

3. ladder   _____

4. suppose   _____

5. burrow   _____

6. middle   _____

7. sitter   _____

8. stirrup   _____

9. summer   _____

10. sudden   _____

11. support   _____

12. swallow   _____

13. valley   _____

14. worry   _____

15. yellow   _____

WORD ANALYSIS   C. 3. *Double consonant*

DIRECTIONS: Read each word and study the way the word is divided into syllables. On the blank line, write <u>Yes</u> if the word is divided into syllables correctly. Write <u>No</u> if the word is not divided into syllables correctly.

1.	fluffy	fluf / fy	_____
2.	wagging	wagg / ing	_____
3.	shaggy	shag / gy	_____
4.	tunnel	tun / nel	_____
5.	grinning	grinn / ing	_____
6.	bubble	bub / ble	_____
7.	message	mes / sage	_____
8.	slipping	slipp / ing	_____
9.	current	cur / rent	_____
10.	pebbles	peb / bles	_____
11.	butter	butt / er	_____
12.	cottage	cot / tage	_____
13.	canned	cann / ed	_____
14.	rotten	rot / ten	_____
15.	dinner	din / ner	_____
16.	comma	com / ma	_____
17.	kitten	kit / ten	_____
18.	rabbit	rab / bit	_____
19.	pattern	pat / tern	_____
20.	cabbage	cab / bage	_____

WORD ANALYSIS   D. Can Hyphenate Words Using Syllable Rules

DIRECTIONS: Hyphenate each of the following words in the space provided as if there were not enough room on the line to write the whole word.

Example: bony   bo
_____   ___
                 ny
                 ___

1. velvet   _____   9. whirring   _____

             _____   _____

2. herring   _____   10. Juno   _____

             _____   _____

3. wedding   _____   11. radish   _____

             _____   _____

4. suppose   _____   12. trotted   _____

             _____   _____

5. water   _____   13. sparrow   _____

             _____   _____

6. solid   _____   14. spoken   _____

             _____   _____

7. tidal   _____   15. doggy   _____

             _____   _____

8. follow   _____

             _____

WORD ANALYSIS   **D. Can Hyphenate Words Using Syllable Rules**

DIRECTIONS: The second column shows each word hyphenated. If the word is hyphenated correctly, write <u>Yes</u>. If the word is not hyphenated correctly, write <u>No</u>.

1. salty	sal-ty	_____
2. rotten	rott-en	_____
3. runner	run-ner	_____
4. sawmill	saw-mill	_____
5. saucer	sau-cer	_____
6. regard	reg-ard	_____
7. road	road	_____
8. lettuce	let-tuce	_____
9. machine	ma-chine	_____
10. marry	mar-ry	_____
11. poison	po-ison	_____
12. contest	con-test	_____
13. herself	her-self	_____
14. reptile	rep-tile	_____
15. forget	forg-et	_____
16. message	mes-sage	_____
17. mason	ma-son	_____
18. measure	mea-sure	_____
19. movie	mo-vie	_____
20. return	re-turn	_____

WORD ANALYSIS   D. Can Hyphenate Words Using Syllable Rules

DIRECTIONS: Study the words in Columns A and B. Circle the word that is hyphenated correctly.

		A	B			A	B
1.	hurry	hur-ry	hurr-y	11.	ill	ill	i-ll
2.	predict	pred-ict	pre-dict	12.	find	fi-nd	find
3.	happen	happe-n	hap-pen	13.	label	la-bel	lab-el
4.	goggles	gog-gles	gogg-les	14.	deer	deer	de-er
5.	return	re-turn	ret-urn	15.	dinner	dinn-er	din-ner
6.	hard	ha-rd	hard	16.	music	mu-sic	mus-ic
7.	fellow	fel-low	fell-ow	17.	happy	hap-py	happ-y
8.	chugging	chu-gging	chug-ging	18.	flippers	flipp-ers	flip-pers
9.	desert	des-ert	de-sert	19.	suffix	suf-fix	suff-ix
10.	crabby	crab-by	cra-bby	20.	ears	e-ars	ears

WORD ANALYSIS   D. Can Hyphenate Words Using Syllable Rules

DIRECTIONS: Hyphenate each of the following words in the space provided. If the word cannot be hyphenated, leave the space blank.

1. word _____

2. yellow _____

3. visit _____

4. valley _____

5. lake _____

6. station _____

7. bottle _____

8. sure _____

9. puppy _____

10. began _____

11. sudden _____

12. police _____

13. sled _____

14. parade _____

15. scissors _____

16. guitar _____

17. middle _____

18. visa _____

19. better _____

20. wet _____

WORD ANALYSIS   D. Can Hyphenate Words Using Syllable Rules

DIRECTIONS: Write each of the following words as if there were not enough room to print the whole word on a line.

Example: channel   <u>   chan-   </u>
                            <u>   nel   </u>

1. pressure   _____   9. water   _____

                _____   _____

2. final   _____   10. offer   _____

                _____   _____

3. puppet   _____   11. lesson   _____

                _____   _____

4. suggest   _____   12. decide   _____

                _____   _____

5. declare   _____   13. polite   _____

                _____   _____

6. shovel   _____   14. travel   _____

                _____   _____

7. mitten   _____   15. report   _____

                _____   _____

8. away   _____

                _____

WORD ANALYSIS   E. Understands Use of Primary Accent Mark

DIRECTIONS: Read each word carefully. If the accent mark is correctly placed, write <u>Yes</u> on the line. If the accent mark is incorrectly placed, write <u>No</u> on the line.

1. sad´- dle   _____

2. pea´- nut   _____

3. ti - ger´   _____

4. fin´- ish   _____

5. a´- way   _____

6. cir´- cus   _____

7. hill´- side   _____

8. teach´- er   _____

9. hob´- by   _____

10. bro - ken´   _____

11. jel´- ly   _____

12. king´- dom   _____

13. la - bel´   _____

14. kit´- ten   _____

15. jum´- bo   _____

WORD ANALYSIS   **E. Understands Use of Primary Accent Mark**

DIRECTIONS: Say each word to yourself and place the accent mark over the syllable where you think it belongs.

1. pupil   pu - pil

2. vowel   vow - el

3. iron   i - ron

4. Jenny   Jen - ny

5. gentle   gen - tle

6. follow   fol - low

7. heavy   heav - y

8. fuzzy   fuzz - y

9. cradle   cra - dle

10. coffee   cof - fee

11. flower   flow - er

12. dinner   din - ner

13. corner   cor - ner

14. happen   hap - pen

15. danger   dan - ger

WORD ANALYSIS   E. Understands Use of Primary Accent Mark

DIRECTIONS: Draw a circle around the word that has the accent mark in the correct place.

	Column A	Column B
1. special	spe´- cial	spe - cial´
2. double	dou - ble´	dou´- ble
3. darkness	dark´- ness	dark - ness´
4. pitcher	pitch´- er	pitch - er´
5. Daddy	Dad´- dy	Dad - dy´
6. careless	care - less´	care´- less
7. captain	cap - tain´	cap´- tain
8. number	num´- ber	num - ber´
9. color	col - or´	col´- or
10. pumpkin	pump´- kin	pump - kin´
11. squirrel	squir´- rel	squir - rel´
12. basket	bas - ket´	bas´- ket
13. garden	gar - den´	gar´- den
14. answer	an - swer´	an´- swer
15. mirror	mir´- ror	mir - ror´

WORD ANALYSIS   E. Understands Use of Primary Accent Mark

DIRECTIONS: Place an accent mark (∕) over the accented syllables.

1. water   wa - ter

2. rubbing   rub - bing

3. yellow   yel - low

4. supper   sup - per

5. angry   an - gry

6. thankful   thank - ful

7. powder   pow - der

8. report   re - port

9. donkey   don - key

10. rabbit   rab - bit

11. wagon   wag - on

12. packing   pack - ing

13. party   par - ty

14. ourselves   our - selves

15. tadpole   tad - pole

WORD ANALYSIS   E. Understands Use of Primary Accent Mark

DIRECTIONS: Say each of these two-syllable words and write 1 if the first syllable is accented or stressed, and 2 if the second syllable is accented.

a. awful	_____	k. measure	_____
b. apple	_____	l. twinkle	_____
c. soda	_____	m. puzzle	_____
d. cabin	_____	n. closet	_____
e. kettle	_____	o. purple	_____
f. sparkle	_____	p. button	_____
g. pencil	_____	q. lemon	_____
h. nutmeg	_____	r. fainted	_____
i. fiddle	_____	s. untie	_____
j. middle	_____	t. lizard	_____

WORD ANALYSIS   **F. Knows to Accent First Syllable Unless It Is a Prefix**

DIRECTIONS: Read the following words and underline the syllable that should receive the primary accent mark.

1. yes - ter - day

2. de - mand

3. sto - ry - tell - er

4. mis - take

5. be - came

6. pre - sume

7. con - crete

8. cou - ple

9. tri - cy - cle

10. wood - chuck

11. cow - boy

12. de - part - ment

13. fall - ing

14. sky - scrap - er

15. hum - mer

16. no - bod - y

17. pre - tend

18. sub - mit

19. Nav - a - ho

20. com - mand

21. tre - men - dous

22. fif - ty

23. thank - ful

24. flag - pole

25. be - head - ed

26. pas - sen - ger

27. el - bow

28. in - tro - duce

29. drip - pings

30. flip - per

Name: _____ Date: _____

DIRECTIONS: Study each word and write <u>Yes</u> if the accent mark is on the correct syllable. Write <u>No</u> if the accent mark is on the wrong syllable.

1. la´- bel _____   11. in - duct´ _____

2. jut - ted´ _____   12. let - ter´ _____

3. re - do´ _____   13. pro - claim´ _____

4. post´- man _____   14. Lin´- da _____

5. com - plete´ _____   15. ex - claim´ _____

6. Grand´- ma _____   16. dis - miss´ _____

7. de´- part _____   17. grand - son´ _____

8. pil´- low _____   18. pre - side´ _____

9. pré´- vent _____   19. pi´- lot _____

10. leak´- y _____   20. ex - am´ _____

WORD ANALYSIS   **F. Knows to Accent First Syllable Unless It Is a Prefix**

DIRECTIONS: Say each word to yourself and circle the word in Column A or B that is accented correctly.

	Column A	Column B
1. pitcher	pitch - er′	pitch′- er
2. odor	o - dor′	o′- dor
3. lemon	lem′- on	lem - on′
4. meow	me - ow′	me′- ow
5. faucet	fau - cet′	fau′- cet
6. plaster	plas′- ter	plas - ter′
7. enjoy	en′- joy	en - joy′
8. improper	im - prop′- er	im′- prop - er
9. chilly	chil′- ly	chil - ly′
10. prefer	pre′- fer	pre - fer′
11. pepper	pep′- per	pep - per′
12. Daddy	Dad - dy′	Dad′- dy
13. impure	im - pure′	im′- pure
14. Monday	Mon - day′	Mon′- day
15. minnow	min′- now	min - now′

WORD ANALYSIS   **F. Knows to Accent First Syllable Unless It Is a Prefix**

DIRECTIONS: Read each word and draw a line under the syllable that is accented.

1. indeed   in - deed

2. goggles   gog - gles

3. noble   no - ble

4. ocean   o - cean

5. perhaps   per - haps

6. hopeless   hope - less

7. transfer   trans - fer

8. abed   a - bed

9. entrust   en - trust

10. discuss   dis - cuss

11. intact   in - tact

12. holly   hol - ly

13. intention   in - ten - tion

14. fossil   fos - sil

15. disarm   dis - arm

WORD ANALYSIS   F. Knows to Accent First Syllable Unless It Is a Prefix

DIRECTIONS: Read each sentence and select the word that will complete the sentence correctly. Write the word in the blank.

1. The knight _____ old and feeble.
   be-came′   be-long′   be-cause′

2. The boys _____ eating watermelon.
   en-joy′   en-cir′-cle   en-roll′

3. The accident happened _____ nine o'clock.
   be-fore′   be-cause′   be-hind′

4. Tom was very _____ when his team lost the game.
   un-wind′   un-hap′-py   un-do′

5. Amy _____ the map and got lost.
   mis-read′   mis-spell′   mis-take′

6. The nurse _____ the book she was reading.
   mis-placed′   mis-spell′   mis-treat′-ed

7. The barber _____ what I said and shaved my head.
   mis-un-der-stood′   mis-take′   mis-deed′

8. The teacher asked the class to _____ their books from their desks.
   re-move′   re-mind′   re-write′

9. Elves come out at night and dance in the _____ .
   moon′-light   ma′-ple   mar′-ket

10. The hunter had to _____ his steps to get out of the woods.
    re-play′   re-tie′   re-trace′

11. The old house was _____ for the new owners.
    re-built′   re-act′   re-load′

12. Linda put her hands in her _____ to keep them warm.
    pock′-ets   pea′-nut   pa′-per

13. The thirsty man asked to have his glass _____ .
    re-turn′   re-act′   re-filled′

14. The string had to be _____ before the package could be opened.
    un-tied′   un-hap′-py   un-a′-ble

15. The sky _____ was gray and gloomy.
    o-ver-head′   o-ver-turn′   o-ver-look′

COMPREHENSION   A. Can Find Main Idea in Story

DIRECTIONS: Read the paragraphs below and answer the questions that follow.

A.   Matilda sat in her rocking chair and was very quiet. A tear slowly ran down her cheek. There was nothing she could do. She had to admit the fact. Matilda could not read the birthday card. She was blind.

B.   Matilda admitted that she was blind, but she was a fighter. She would not give up. She would not consider a life without books and magazines. Yes, she was blind, but she would find an answer to her problem.

C.   With a great deal of courage, she looked for a school where she could learn Braille. Braille is a way in which the blind use their finger tips to read a kind of print that is on top of a page. At age 75, Matilda went back to school. For many months, she went to class every day. It was very hard work.

D.   Then came the day when Matilda was able to read with her fingers and with no help from the teacher. She felt very proud. At her age, she had learned a new skill. She now reads books and magazines every day.

Write the letter of the paragraph beside the sentence below that tells its main idea.

_____ 1. Matilda went to school.

_____ 2. Matilda realizes she is blind.

_____ 3. Matilda is a very brave fighter.

_____ 4. Matilda learns to read with her finger tips.

Put a check mark (✓) next to the best title for this story.

_____ 5. Books and Fingers
_____ 6. Brave Lady
_____ 7. Seeing Eye Dogs

COMPREHENSION   A. Can Find Main Idea in Story

DIRECTIONS: Put a check mark (V) next to the sentence that tells the main idea of each paragraph.

Hawaii is an unusual state. It is made up of 132 islands with deep blue water between them. These islands were formed by volcanoes rising from the ocean floor. Many brightly colored flowers, graceful palm trees, and other beautiful plants grow on the islands.

1. _____ a. Hawaii is an island.
   _____ b. Hawaii is an unusual state.
   _____ c. Hawaii is a state.

Hawaii is the name of the largest of the islands. It was formed by five volcanoes. Three of the volcanoes are inactive and two volcanoes are still active. These are sometimes called "drive-in" volcanoes because one can drive up close to see them. When one of the volcanoes erupts, it provides spectacular fireworks.

2. _____ a. Hawaii was formed by volcanoes.
   _____ b. Hawaii has two active volcanoes.
   _____ c. Hawaii means volcanoes.

Maui is another one of Hawaii's islands. This island was formed by two volcanoes. It has a large crater which was formed by wind erosion. The crater is filled with cinder cones from one of the volcanoes.

3. _____ a. Maui is a cinder cone.
   _____ b. Maui is a Hawaiian island.
   _____ c. Maui is an active volcano.

The Garden Island of Hawaii is Kauai. This island was discovered by Captain Cook. The island was built by one very large volcano. It has many beautiful plants, flowers, streams, canyons, and waterfalls on it. To see this island is to love it.

4. _____ a. Kauai is called the Garden Island.
   _____ b. Kauai is named for Captain Cook.
   _____ c. There is an old island named Kauai.

5. The best title for this page would be:
   _____ a. Volcanoes
   _____ b. Beautiful Hawaii
   _____ c. Greenery

COMPREHENSION   **A. Can Find Main Idea in Story**

DIRECTIONS: Put a check mark (V) next to the phrase that tells the main idea of each paragraph.

A.   Snow, snow, snow, oh the beautiful snow! There is no more beautiful sight than large, white snowflakes falling. Snow falls quietly and softly. Falling snow is like an angel's wing brushing the earth with paint. Snow is peaceful and gentle and touches everything.

_____ 1. Snow is an angel
_____ 2. Snowflakes
_____ 3. Snow is beautiful

B.   Boys and girls get excited when they see snow falling. Snow means happy times and fun days. Snow sometimes means a day out of school and a day for play. Snow means sliding, skiing, and snowballs. Snow means making snow angels and snow ice cream. Snow means playing till your nose gets red and your cheeks tingle.

_____ 1. Fun days for boys and girls
_____ 2. Don'ts for a snowy day
_____ 3. Snow gives you a red nose

C.   Mothers look at snow and think of warm things. Mothers think of sweaters, boots, mittens, gloves, hats, and warm coats. Mothers know that children playing in the snow come home cold, wet, and hungry. Warm soup and hot chocolate taste good on cold, snowy days.

_____ 1. Cold days
_____ 2. A recipe for warm soup
_____ 3. Mothers' thoughts for snowy days

D.   Fathers look at falling snow and think of shovels, salt, stuck automobiles, and snowdrifts. As soon as the snow stops, the walks must be cleaned. Shoveling snow is difficult work but it must be done. Snow means chains for tires and driving slowly. Snow means snowplows and snowdrifts.

_____ 1. Snowplows and snowdrifts
_____ 2. Fathers and snow
_____ 3. Shoveling snow

E.   The best title for this story is:
_____ 1. No School Today
_____ 2. Snow
_____ 3. Fathers and Snow
_____ 4. Mothers and Snow

COMPREHENSION   A. Can Find Main Idea in Story

DIRECTIONS: Read each of the following paragraphs and then write the letter of each paragraph beside the phrase below that tells its main idea.

A.   The 1980 Winter Olympic games were held in Lake Placid, New York. The opening ceremonies occurred on February 13, for the thirteenth time in modern history. A total of 1200 athletes from forty countries all around the world took part. Hundreds of millions of people watched the ceremonies and events on television. More than 51,000 people attended the games.

B.   The first Winter Olympics were held in France in 1924, with barely 300 'athletes. Four years later, in 1928, they were held in Switzerland. The United States hosted the winter games for the first time in 1928. The Winter Olympics have also been held in Japan, Austria, Norway, and Italy.

C.   Every athlete in the Winter Olympics wants to win a gold medal. Not everyone can win. But everyone who takes part in the games returns home knowing that he or she has competed against the best. Every athlete must practice for many hours a day and for many months in order to compete. To be in the games is a great honor.

D.   Some of the events in the Winter Olympics are figure skating, speed skating, ice hockey, tobogganing, two-man and four-man bobsledding, downhill skiing, ski jumping, and cross-country skiing. A very dangerous event is the slalom, in which skiers make two runs down a twisting ski course marked by colored poles. The person with the fastest time wins. The winners must be fast, brave, and willing to work hard.

_____ 1. Winter Olympic games

_____ 2. Places the games have been held

_____ 3. 1980 Winter Olympics

_____ 4. Olympic athletes

5. The best title for this story would be:

_____ A. Athletes Work Hard

_____ B. The Winter Olympics

_____ C. Gold Medals

COMPREHENSION   **A. Can Find Main Idea in Story**

DIRECTIONS: Put a check mark (**√**) next to the phrase that tells the main idea of each of the following paragraphs.

Marguerite and Lisa were getting ready to go on a vacation with their mother at the beach. Each girl sat down and made a list of all the things she wanted to take with her. When their lists were finished, they pulled suitcases out of the closet and started to pack.

1. _____ a. Getting ready for a vacation
   _____ b. The beach
   _____ c. Making a list

In her suitcase, Marguerite packed jeans, T-shirts, bathing suit, tennis shoes, socks, and underwear. Then she looked for her Frisbee and beach ball. Lisa packed her suitcase and made doubly sure that she had her new bathing suit. Soon both girls were ready. They waited for their mother to come home from work so that they could leave.

2. _____ a. Waiting for Mother
   _____ b. Packing for the trip
   _____ c. Frisbee and beach ball

As soon as Mother drove into the carport, Marguerite and Lisa carried their suitcases out to the car and helped to put them into the trunk. They wanted to leave right away. Mother told the girls that they would have to wait a few minutes while she packed a few things for herself and made some sandwiches to eat on the trip. The girls offered to help and then ran to the kitchen to start making the sandwiches.

3. _____ a. Helping Mother get ready
   _____ b. Putting suitcases in the car
   _____ c. Making sandwiches

Mother placed her suitcase in the trunk and then got into the car. Lisa and Marguerite shouted as the car backed out of the carport into the street. At last they were on their way to the beach! After a short time, the girls fell asleep. Mother drove and drove. The trip took three hours. When they arrived at the beach motel, Mother woke the girls. They could not believe the trip had been so short. They hadn't even had a chance to eat!

4. _____ a. Falling asleep
   _____ b. The motel
   _____ c. A trip to the beach

5. The best title for this story would be:
   _____ a. Going on Vacation
   _____ b. Packing a Suitcase
   _____ c. A Short Trip

III

COMPREHENSION   **B. Can Keep Events in Proper Sequence**

DIRECTIONS: Read each story and then place the numbers 1, 2, 3, and 4 in front of the phrases to show the order in which the events occurred in the story.

A.   Jo Ann went to the kitchen to make a sandwich for lunch. She opened the bread box, placed a loaf on the cutting board, and cut two pieces of fresh bread. Jo Ann then spread peanut butter on one slice of bread and apple jelly on the other slice of bread. She licked her lips as she thought of how good the sandwich would taste. Then she cut the sandwich and began to eat.

_____ . Spread the peanut butter   _____ Took the bread out

_____ Began to eat   _____ Spread the jelly

B.   "Oh, what a great day for fishing!" John thought as he jumped out of bed. He and his big brother, Tom, were going to Indian Lake for the day. He grabbed his jeans and dressed very fast. John checked to see if Tom was up. Then he went to the kitchen to prepare his breakfast. He whistled because he was happy.

_____ Grabbed his jeans   _____ Checked to see if Tom was up

_____ Went to the kitchen

_____ Jumped out of bed

C.   The radio announcer repeated many times that the snow would continue to fall all day. Dad was getting ready to go to work. He put on his warmest sweater and then his jacket. He wrapped a wool scarf around his neck, put on his boots, coat, cap, and earmuffs. Dad then picked up his gloves and unlocked the door to go out.

_____ Put on his jacket   _____ Picked up his gloves

_____ Put on his boots   _____ Was getting ready to go to work

D.   Danny sat down and began his homework. He wanted to go out to play so he wasted no time. Danny opened his book and pulled out a sheet of paper. He wrote his name on the paper and copied the arithmetic problems. Then he started doing the problems. Thirty minutes later he finished the last one. Danny closed the book, jumped up, and shouted. The boys were outside waiting for him to play ball.

_____ Jumped up and shouted   _____ Copied the problems

_____ Did the homework   _____ Opened the book

COMPREHENSION   B. Can Keep Events in Proper Sequence

DIRECTIONS: Read each paragraph and then number the sentences beneath it in the order in which they happened.

A.   Today was Mother's birthday. Phillip decided that a birthday cake for Mother would be a nice surprise. He took out the mixing bowl and a package of cake mix. The directions seemed easy enough. One of the first things he did was to prepare the cake pans and turn the oven on to 350°. When the cake mix was ready, he poured the mix into the pans and placed the pans in the oven.

_____ Read the directions
_____ Took out the cake mix package
_____ Prepared the cake mix
_____ Put the cake pans into the oven

B.   Phillip set the oven timer and waited for the cake to bake. At long last, the timer rang. He opened the oven door and saw that the cakes looked great. Using potholders, he slowly took the cakes out of the oven and placed them on the cake rack to cool. Ten minutes later the cakes were cool enough to be taken out of the pans. Phillip was getting more excited every minute. The cakes did not stick to the pans and were now on the rack cooling.

_____ Timer rang   _____ Set timer
_____ Cakes cooling   _____ Placed cakes on rack

C.   Phillip wondered what kind of frosting to put on the cakes. He knew that Mother liked chocolate frosting. He got the right box down from the shelf and followed the directions on the back of the box. After putting butter and water into the mix, he beat the frosting till it was smooth. He put some frosting on the cool cakes, placed one cake layer on top of the other, and finished putting on the frosting.

_____ Beat the frosting
_____ Frosted the cake
_____ Followed the directions on the box
_____ Got the box of frosting mix down from the shelf

D.   The cake was beautiful. Phillip wondered if there were any candles in the cabinet. Yes, today was his lucky day. He took out the candles and put them on the cake. He placed the cake in the middle of the kitchen table. Phillip was feeling very proud of himself. He was eager for his mother to come home.

_____ Put candles on the cake   _____ Looked for candles
_____ Felt proud   _____ Placed the cake on the table

COMPREHENSION   B. Can Keep Events in Proper Sequence

DIRECTIONS: Read the stories and number the sentences in the order in which they happen.

A.   Valentine's Day was in three days and Agnes had five cents. Agnes wanted to have valentines for her mother, father, grandparents, brother, and sisters. What could she do with five cents? It was not enough to buy valentines. What could five cents buy?

Suddenly, Agnes had a thought. Her valentines would be very special and no one would have any others like them. Her family would get cards designed by Agnes.

Out came the paper, scissors, glue, and crayons. Agnes got to work and designed cards. It was hard work making a special card for each member of the family. Agnes worked and worked. The cards began to take shape. In about an hour, the red and white cards with hearts and flowers were finished. She knew that her family would be pleased because no one else would have a card like the ones she had made.

_____ Getting an idea
_____ Making valentines
_____ Thinking of Valentine's Day
_____ Feeling happy when the work was done

B.   Chris hung up the phone and told his mother that Dr. Allen had asked him to feed Heidi while she was away. Chris was happy to have the job. Dr. Allen paid him well to feed and water Heidi.

The following night at six o'clock, Chris went next door. Heidi was happy to see him. She jumped up on him and almost knocked him over. Heidi was a large German shepherd puppy. Chris picked up the dog bowl and went to the storeroom to get the dog food. He filled up the bowl and went into the back yard. He put the bowl on the ground. Next, Chris refilled the water pail.

Once these things were done, Chris took time to play with Heidi. Heidi loved to chase the ball and bring it back. Chris wished he had a dog like Heidi. It began to get dark. Chris knew it was time to go home. He patted Heidi and went out through the gate. Chris made sure that the gate was closed so Heidi could not get out.

_____ Chris closes the gate.
_____ The dog is fed.
_____ Chris gets a job.
_____ Chris plays with Heidi.

COMPREHENSION   B. Can Keep Events in Proper Sequence

DIRECTIONS: Number (1, 2, 3, 4) the events in the order in which they would probably happen.

A. Going on a fishing trip
____ Get into the car and drive.
____ Plan the trip.
____ Go fishing.
____ Pack a suitcase.

B. Going to school
____ Eat breakfast.
____ Get out of bed and get dressed.
____ Walk to school.
____ Say good morning to the teacher.

C. Buying candy at the store
____ Eat the candy.
____ Decide what to buy.
____ Look over the candy at the store.
____ Pay for the candy.

D. Getting ready for a party
____ Go to the party.
____ Take a bath.
____ Have fun at the party.
____ Get dressed.

E. Going ice skating
____ Ask Dad if you can go skating.
____ Put on the ice skates.
____ Put on warm clothes.
____ Walk to the pond.

F. Making candy
____ Leave the candy to cool.
____ Take out sugar, cream, cocoa, and butter.
____ Find a candy recipe.
____ Cook the candy.

G. Cutting the grass
____ Cut the grass.
____ Get out the mower.
____ Check out the mower.
____ Put the machine away.

H. Making a telephone call
____ Pick up the phone.
____ Dial the number.
____ Wait while the phone rings.
____ Get the correct phone number.

I. Sending a letter
____ Seal the envelope.
____ Write the letter.
____ Mail the letter.
____ Put the letter in the envelope.

J. Taking a test
____ Study before the test.
____ Finish the test.
____ Go to the classroom.
____ Follow the teacher's directions.

COMPREHENSION   **B. Can Keep Events in Proper Sequence**

DIRECTIONS: Number the sentences in the order in which they happen.

A.   It was time to put the Christmas tree up in the den. Once the tree was in the stand, the decorations would come out. Mother always put the decorations on the tree in a set order. First, Dad would put the lights on the tree. The children would then put on the ornaments. Mother saved the job of putting the tinsel on for last. Then everyone would admire the tree.

_____ Putting on the tinsel   _____ Putting the tree in the stand
_____ Putting lights on the tree   _____ Putting on the ornaments

B.   Grandma and Grandpa were coming for Thanksgiving dinner. Kathryn was helping Mother set the table. The table was covered with a pretty cloth. A candle was placed in the center of the table. Kathryn set the knives, forks, and spoons in each place. Mother helped her with the dinner plates. A glass was placed above everyone's knife.

_____ A candle was placed in the center.
_____ Knives, forks, and spoons were put on the table.
_____ Glasses were placed above the knife.
_____ A cloth was put on the table.

C.   The girls had been promised an Easter egg hunt by their scout leader. Everyone helped to make the party a success. Mothers boiled the eggs. The girls painted the eggs and the scout leader hid them. Now it was time to hunt for the eggs. The girl who found the most eggs would be the winner. Each girl was given a basket. When the leader said "Go," the hunt began.

_____ The eggs were cooked.   _____ The hunt began.
_____ The eggs were hidden.   _____ The eggs were painted.

D.   Freddie got up very early. It was the day of the Fourth of July picnic. This holiday meant fried chicken, baseball games, and fireworks. Freddie listened and heard his mother in the kitchen. He knew that at ten o'clock they would leave for the park. He flew out of bed. Freddie helped his dad put everything in the car. He packed his baseball cap and glove.

_____ Freddie took his baseball cap and glove.
_____ It was the Fourth of July.
_____ Freddie helped his dad.
_____ Mother was in the kitchen.

COMPREHENSION   C. Can Draw Logical Conclusions

DIRECTIONS: Read each paragraph and place an X in front of the best answer.

Tim skated as fast as he could. He zipped over the ice. His coach was watching the clock. He had to take a minute off his time.

1. Tim was in a
   ____ a. race
   ____ b. play
   ____ c. dance

2. To win, Tim has to improve his
   ____ a. skates
   ____ b. watch
   ____ c. speed

Beth looked at the pieces. She was heartbroken. As she was setting the kitchen table, the cup had fallen to the floor. What would Mother say when she learned of the good china cup accident?

3. Beth was in the
   ____ a. kitchen
   ____ b. bedroom
   ____ c. patio

4. She was feeling
   ____ a. happy
   ____ b. surprised
   ____ c. uneasy

The cake smelled delicious. It was time to take the cake out of the pan. Peggy picked up the cake pan and turned it over on the cake rack. Peggy turned white. What could she do now?

5. The cake
   ____ a. fell apart
   ____ b. came out of the pan
   ____ c. the phone rang

6. Peggy turned white because she was
   ____ a. happy
   ____ b. worried
   ____ c. sleepy

Chris took the money and walked home. He had been feeding a neighbor's horse. The extra money came in handy. He wondered if he should save the money for a bicycle or spend it on a basketball.

7. Chris was trying to reach
   ____ a. the neighbor
   ____ b. a decision
   ____ c. the horse

8. Chris had a
   ____ a. bicycle
   ____ b. basketball
   ____ c. job

The alarm rang. Joe jumped out of bed and ran to the window. The sun was shining. It was a beautiful day. He put on his jeans and grabbed his fishing rod.

9. Joe was
   ____ a. happy
   ____ b. sad
   ____ c. serious

10. It was
   ____ a. evening
   ____ b. lunch-time
   ____ c. morning

COMPREHENSION   C. Can Draw Logical Conclusions

DIRECTIONS: Read each group of words and place an X in front of the word that fits best.

1. basketball, football, soccer, tennis

__ a. sports   __ b. dance   __ c. music   __ d. art

2. graceful, ballerina, music, form

__ a. orchestra   __ b. football   __ c. sports   __ d. dance

3. quarterback, long rectangular field, goal posts, halfback

__ a. baseball   __ b. basketball __ c. football   __ d. tennis

4. water, lanes, suits, towels

__ a. gymnasium   __ b. swimming __ c. tennis   __ d. polo

5. ice, skates, puck, stick

__ a. sledding   __ b. skiing   __ c. roller skating   __ d. hockey

6. harp, violins, bugles, clarinets

__ a. orchestra   __ b. stadium   __ c. train   __ d. boxing

7. clowns, acrobats, elephants, tigers

__ a. play   __ b. zoo   __ c. circus   __ d. rodeo

8. tent, fire, sleeping bag, lantern

__ a. tennis   __ b. camping   __ c. canoeing __ d. swimming

9. snow, ice, wind, sleet

__ a. tornado   __ b. summer   __ c. spring   __ d. storm

10. paintings, pottery, sculpture, drawings

__ a. sports   __ b. dance   __ c. art   __ d. music

COMPREHENSION   C. Can Draw Logical Conclusions

DIRECTIONS: Draw a circle around the letter in front of the best answer.

Heidi jumped on Al and put her big paws on his jacket. Al pushed her down and played with her. He threw a stick. Heidi ran to get it.

1. Heidi is a
   a. cat   b. turtle   c. dog
2. Heidi likes to
   a. play   b. eat   c. work

The lightning lit up the sky. The thunder roared like hundreds of lions. The rain was falling in thick sheets. The car barely moved.

3. The driver was being
   a. careless   b. careful   c. foolish
4. The night was
   a. pleasant   b. unusual   c. calm

The team was excited. The best players were on the field. There were only two minutes left to play. The winner would be number one.

5. The team was
   a. winning   b. losing   c. calm
6. The game was
   a. beginning   b. ending   c. at midpoint

Cal wiped his forehead. It was hot in the sun. The work was only half done and he wanted to play now that school was out.

7. It is
   a. fall   b. winter   c. summer
8. Cal has
   a. a job   b. school   c. time to play

The bags of leaves were lined up by the street. Lee put the rake and other tools away. It had been hard work, but the yard was clean of leaves.

9. The time of year is
   a. spring   b. summer   c. fall
10. Lee felt
   a. unhappy   b. worried   c. proud

COMPREHENSION·   C. Can Draw Logical Conclusions

DIRECTIONS: Put an X in front of the best answer to each question.

1. The basketball team had two minutes left to play. The score was tied. The team had to play the very best it could to win. What should the coach do?

_____ a. Let the best players play.

_____ b. Let all the players have a turn to play for one minute each.

_____ c. Let the players who were sitting on the bench play.

2. The skaters were practicing for the Olympics. They wanted to win a gold medal for speed skating. The coach had the skaters race around the rink. What was the coach doing as the skaters raced?

_____ a. The coach took a coffee break.

_____ b. The coach read a paper.

_____ c. The coach timed the players and watched carefully.

3. As the skaters lined up for the race, the crowd became very quiet. Tom was nervous, but he kept saying, "I can win, I can win." The judge said, "At the sound of the gun, begin." What do you think happened next?

_____ a. The judge fainted.

_____ b. The gun went off.

_____ c. Tom fell.

4. The girls dove into the pool and swam toward the other end. Every second counted. The people shouted. The winner would receive the gold medal. What were the judges doing?

_____ a. The judges were swimming.

_____ b. The judges were shouting.

_____ c. The judges were timing the swimmers.

5. This was the day when Harris would have his first tennis lesson. He raced over to the tennis court. Harris had a new tennis racket and balls. He did not want to be late. How did Harris feel?

_____ a. Harris was angry.

_____ b. Harris was excited and nervous.

_____ c. Harris was calm.

COMPREHENSION   C. Can Draw Logical Conclusions

DIRECTIONS: Read each group of words and draw an X through the word that does not belong.

1. star
   sky
   moon
   night
   bird

2. skates
   ice
   winter
   flowers
   cold

3. tent
   sleeping bag
   lantern
   home
   camp

4. horse
   hoof
   silk
   brush
   feed

5. house
   store
   yard
   grass
   fence

6. flower
   mouse
   seed
   stem
   petal

7. wash
   water
   bread
   soap
   towel

8. teeth
   brush
   dentist
   candy
   toothpaste

9. cabin
   mountains
   rocks
   climb
   milk

10. bird
    glasses
    wings
    beak
    fly

11. homework
    book
    dark
    pencil
    paper

12. candle
    house
    light
    match
    burn

13. phone
    call
    candle
    talk
    friend

14. car
    gas
    paper
    tires
    engine

15. bear
    eat
    brown
    animal
    large

16. breakfast
    juice
    noon
    eggs
    milk

COMPREHENSION   D. Can See Relationships

DIRECTIONS: Put an X in front of the word that best completes each sentence.

1. Moon is to night as sun is to
   ___ spring   ___ dinner   ___ day

2. Pencil is to paper as type is to
   ___ book   ___ fire   ___ water

3. Hay is to cows as seed is to
   ___ bears   ___ birds   ___ fish

4. Eggs are to bacon as cream is to
   ___ coffee   ___ ham   ___ syrup

5. Cold is to winter as hot is to
   ___ autumn   ___ summer   ___ fall

6. Teacher is to school as nurse is to
   ___ hospital   ___ hotel   ___ motel

7. Turkey is to Thanksgiving as rabbits are to
   ___ Easter   ___ Christmas   ___ New Year's

8. Tire is to car as propeller is to
   ___ trailer   ___ train   ___ plane

9. Soil is to plant as water is to
   ___ bird   ___ fish   ___ mule

10. Mitt is to ball as rod is to
    ___ hunt   ___ fish   ___ boat

11. Television is to eye as radio is to
    ___ ear   ___ nose   ___ mouth

12. Sink is to kitchen as tub is to
    ___ bed   ___ bathroom   ___ chair

13. Seven is to eight as twelve is to
    ___ five   ___ sixteen   ___ thirteen

14. Stop is to go as run is to
    ___ ski   ___ walk   ___ skate

15. Voice is to ear as smell is to
    ___ nose   ___ eye   ___ mouth

16. Pillow is to bed as chair is to
    ___ dresser   ___ sofa   ___ table

COMPREHENSION   D. Can See Relationships

DIRECTIONS: Read each pair of sentences carefully. Fill in the blank with the word that best completes the second sentence in each pair.

1. Children need food.

   Automobiles need _____.

2. Birds fly.

   People _____.

3. Footballs are kicked.

   Golf balls are _____.

4. Airplanes move in the sky.

   Fish move in the _____.

5. Girls wear skirts.

   Boys wear _____.

6. Kings live in palaces.

   Horses live in _____.

7. Christmas colors are red and green.

   Halloween colors are _____ and _____.

8. A teacher writes on a chalkboard.

   A secretary works at a _____ .

9. A telephone is used to talk.

   A pen is used to _____.

10. An oar moves a rowboat.

    A fin moves a _____.

11. Pins and needles are used to sew.

    Spoons and bowls are used to _____.

COMPREHENSION   D. Can See Relationships

DIRECTIONS: Place an X in front of the word that is closest in relationship to the first word in each line.

1. under _____ below _____ above _____ close

2. beside _____ on _____ near _____ above

3. over _____ next _____ above _____ below

4. top _____ lowest point _____ highest point _____ middle point

5. beginning _____ first _____ middle _____ end

6. before _____ end _____ behind _____ ahead

7. here _____ below _____ in this spot _____ there

8. back _____ toward the rear _____ toward the front _____ toward the middle

9. bottom _____ lowest point _____ highest point _____ middle point

10. behind _____ end _____ back _____ ahead

11. far _____ a short way off _____ a long way off _____ here

12. below _____ in a low place _____ in a high place _____ in a middle place

13. last _____ beginning _____ middle _____ end

14. between _____ beginning _____ last _____ middle

15. inside _____ up _____ within _____ outside

16. down _____ from high to low _____ from low to high _____ up

17. first _____ beginning _____ end _____ last

18. end _____ first _____ stop _____ middle

19. middle _____ beginning _____ end _____ halfway

20. front _____ ahead _____ behind _____ end

COMPREHENSION   **D. Can See Relationships**

DIRECTIONS: Place an X in front of the word that is closest in relationship to the first word in each line.

1. first   ___ beginning   ___ middle   ___ late

2. after   ___ now   ___ then   ___ never

3. never   ___ at some time   ___ at no time   ___ soon

4. always   ___ forever   ___ never   ___ sometimes

5. end   ___ begin   ___ stop   ___ middle

6. beginning   ___ last   ___ middle   ___ first

7. soon   ___ before long   ___ never   ___ at first

8. early   ___ late   ___ ahead of time   ___ never

9. now   ___ at this moment   ___ yesterday   ___ tomorrow

10. forever   ___ now   ___ always   ___ seldom

11. last   ___ end   ___ now   ___ today

12. then   ___ next   ___ never   ___ end

13. late   ___ on time   ___ end   ___ tardy

14. next   ___ top   ___ beside   ___ bottom

COMPREHENSION   D. Can See Relationships

DIRECTIONS: Place an X in front of the word that best completes the sentence.

1. Fire is to heat as ice is to
   ___ cold   ___ warm   ___ house

2. Igloo is to Eskimo as tent is to
   ___ dancer   ___ Indian   ___ king

3. Time is to clock as temperature is to
   ___ watch   ___ odometer   ___ thermometer

4. Garage is to car as hangar is to
   ___ boat   ___ airplane   ___ bicycle

5. Film is to camera as air is to
   ___ tire   ___ pillow   ___ car

6. Animals are to zoo as paintings are to
   ___ capitol   ___ carnival   ___ museum

7. Peanuts are to elephants as fish are to
   ___ tigers   ___ seals   ___ monkeys

8. Ketchup is to hamburgers as mustard is to
   ___ hot dogs   ___ pancakes   ___ cake

9. Cakes are to birthdays as candy canes are to
   ___ Halloween   ___ Christmas   ___ Thanksgiving

10. Robin is to spring as falling leaves are to
    ___ fall   ___ winter   ___ summer

11. Sister is to brother as mother is to
    ___ cousin   ___ father   ___ nephew

12. Question mark is to question as period is to
    ___ question   ___ sentence   ___ story

13. Squeak is to mouse as moo is to
    ___ horse   ___ pig   ___ cow

14. Carrot is to rabbit as hay is to
    ___ owl   ___ horse   ___ chicken

COMPREHENSION   **E. Can Predict Outcomes**

DIRECTIONS: Read each paragraph and write an answer of your own on the lines underneath it. Remember, several outcomes may make sense.

1. Tom had been told that ghosts lived in the old King house. He didn't really believe the story. Tom slowly opened the creaking door. Suddenly, ... What happens next?

_____

_____

2. Kathryn stood waiting for the school bus. The bus usually came promptly at 7:30. Today, it was 8:00 and the bus had not come. What could be the reason?

_____

_____

3. Whenever Chuck had gone fishing near the old oak tree along the river, he had always caught several large fish. Today, he had been fishing for three hours and all he had gotten were two little fish. What do you suppose had happened?

_____

_____

4. Marguerite went walking every morning at 5:30. She always saw the paper girl delivering the morning paper. Today, Marguerite returned home at 6:30 without seeing the paper girl. What do you suppose had happened?

_____

_____

5. Mutt, Josie's dog, was standing by the back door. His back paws were splattered with red paint. What do you suppose had happened?

_____

_____

COMPREHENSION   **E. Can Predict Outcomes**

DIRECTIONS: Read each paragraph and write an answer of your own on the lines underneath it. Remember, several outcomes are possible.

1. Mother put the cake pans in the oven and started to clean the dirty dishes. As she turned, she saw the eggs on the table. What can you imagine Mother did next?

   _____

   _____

2. Father went to start up his car to go to work. He turned the car key and put his foot on the gas. What do you imagine happened?

   _____

   _____

3. Larry went camping with his father. They slept in the tent. In the middle of the night, Larry was awakened by a loud crash near the campfire. What do you imagine could have caused the loud crash?

   _____

   _____

4. Hans enjoyed ice skating. One day while he was skating, he suddenly fell and his knee was under him. He tried to get up but the pain was horrible. What do you imagine had happened?

   _____

   _____

5. The circus was in town. Robbie was helping the animal trainer feed and water the elephants. Robbie had been working for several hours. Why do you imagine Robbie was working?

   _____

   _____

COMPREHENSION   **E. Can Predict Outcomes**

DIRECTIONS: Read each paragraph and write an answer of your own on the lines underneath it. Remember, several outcomes are possible.

1. The horse ran around the pasture wildly. His mane was flying and so was his tail. He stopped suddenly and snorted. What do you think happened next?

   _____

   _____

2. Phillip sneezed, coughed, and wiped his running eyes. Mother took one look at him and ordered him to go to bed. Ten minutes later, Mother walked into his room and said ... What do you think Phillip's mother said?

   _____

   _____

3. Sandra held her camera and asked everyone to look at her. She said, "When I count to three, everybody please smile. One, two, three ... " What do you imagine happened next?

   _____

   _____

4. Greg went to the storeroom to fill his dog's bowl with Ritzy Dog Chow. He opened the bag of dog food. He looked inside and gasped. He couldn't believe his eyes. What do you imagine Greg saw?

   _____

   _____

5. Lillian was ten years old. Her grandfather gave her a small red box tied with a yellow ribbon. She untied the ribbon, opened the box, and shouted ... What do you imagine Lillian shouted and why?

   _____

   _____

COMPREHENSION   E. Can Predict Outcomes

DIRECTIONS: Read the paragraph. Put an X in front of the answer that is most logical.

1. Mother said, "Heavens! It's 28° outside. This must be the coldest day of the year. It will feel good to get out of the cold."

_____ a. Mother is in the house.   _____ c. Mother is outdoors.
_____ b. Mother is in the car.

2. Mother said, "Tom, you were very kind to thank Uncle Ray for the catcher's mitt. Your thoughtfulness pleased Uncle Ray. I am very proud of you."

_____ a. Mother is angry with Tom.   _____ c. It's Mother's birthday.
_____ b. Mother is happy with Tom.

3. In some countries the people speak many languages. The language of one part of the country may be very different from the language of another part. Some languages are very smooth and pleasant. Other languages are harsh and not so pleasant to the ear.

_____ a. People in some countries may have trouble understanding one another.
_____ b. In some countries all of the people speak the same language.
_____ c. Some people use sign language.

4. When a bird lands, it has to be careful that it doesn't tumble forward. A bird, like an airplane, lands into the wind. The wind acts as a brake. Some birds fan their tails and turn them downward. Their legs absorb much of the shock.

_____ a. Birds land into the wind.
_____ b. Birds use their legs to land.
_____ c. Birds overshoot their landing spot.

5. It was Susan's birthday. The boys and girls from her class were having a party. There was ice cream, cake, and balloons. Suddenly, a loud noise was heard.

_____ a. Susan dropped a dish.   _____ c. The ice cream melted.
_____ b. A balloon burst.

6. The ball game was tied. George was the best kicker on the team. There was only one minute left to play. The coach whispered in George's ear. George went back to his teammates. The team lined up. The ball was passed back, and George kicked. The crowd roared.

_____ a. George missed the posts.   _____ c. George missed the kick.
_____ b. George scored the winning points.

COMPREHENSION   E. Can Predict Outcomes

DIRECTIONS: Read the paragraph. Put an X in front of the answer that makes the best sentence.

1. Ann was going to the store. She would get something good to eat. It came in many colors. It was very cold and tasted extra good on hot days. Ann was going to buy:

_____ a. shoes
_____ b. ice cream
_____ c. a book

2. Cecile couldn't find her lunch. She didn't have time to go back home. Then she saw her twin sister, who told her to sit with her at lunchtime. Cecile's twin would:

_____ a. go and get her lunch for her
_____ b. feel sad
_____ c. share her lunch

3. The sharp-eyed eagle was sitting high up in a tree. It looked around and around. The eagle was hunting for something. It saw a rabbit hop out of its hole. The eagle came down fast. The eagle:
_____ a. liked mushrooms
_____ b. was hunting for something to eat
_____ c. flew away

4. Sandra put a kettle of soup on the stove. Next, she turned up the heat under the kettle. The telephone rang, so she hurried to answer it. She talked and talked and forgot all about the soup. The soup:
_____ a. boiled over
_____ b. got cold
_____ c. was split pea soup

5. Marguerite went into the bathroom to take a bath. She started running the water. Just then the telephone rang. Before she left the bathroom, Marguerite turned the water off. Marguerite was:
_____ a. absent-minded
_____ b. careful
_____ c. lazy

6. Marianne was excited. She counted the days till school would end. Marianne was going to fly to New York to visit her aunt. She had never been on a plane before and she was wondering what it would be like. Marianne is:
_____ a. excited   _____ c. silly
_____ b. calm

COMPREHENSION   F. Can Follow Printed Directions

DIRECTIONS: Read sentence <u>a</u> and do what sentence <u>b</u> tells you to do.

1. a. Tom and Jerry are burning leaves.
   b. Make a box around the word that tells what the boys are burning.

2. a. The Rams are playing the Jets.
   b. Draw a circle around the first team in the sentence.

3. a. My bicycle was damaged in the accident.
   b. Draw an X through what was damaged.

4. a. The wolf came running out of the woods.
   b. Make a box around the word that tells where the wolf was.

5. a. A cactus is a desert shrub.
   b. Underline the word that tells where a cactus grows.

6. a. There's a hole in the sole of my left sneaker.
   b. Draw two lines under the word for a kind of shoe.

7. a. The train arrived at the station twenty minutes late.
   b. Draw a circle around the word that tells where the train is.

8. a. My tooth is giving me much pain.
   b. Write the word that tells what is causing pain: _____

9. a. Maria's favorite dessert is vanilla ice cream.
   b. Draw an X through the person's name.

10. a. Terry ate a grilled cheese sandwich for lunch.
    b. Draw two lines under the words for the kind of sandwich Terry ate.

COMPREHENSION   **F. Can Follow Printed Directions**

DIRECTIONS: There are three shapes at the top of the page. Read and
follow directions.

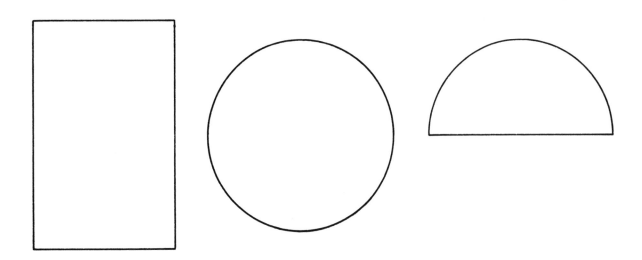

1. Put an A in the middle of the circle.
2. Place an X under the half-circle.
3. Draw a line in the middle of the box from the top to the bottom.
4. Put an R on the right-hand side of the box.
5. Write the word TOP just above the circle.
6. Put a Y inside the half-circle.
7. Divide the circle into four equal parts.
8. Put the number 4 under the box.
9. Draw an apple on the inside of the left side of the box.
10. Place a Z above the half-circle.
11. Write the word BOTTOM at the correct spot below the circle.
12. Draw straight lines up and down in the bottom half of the circle.

COMPREHENSION   **F. Can Follow Printed Directions**

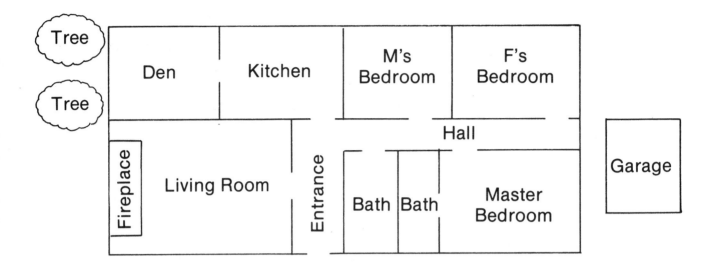

DIRECTIONS:

1. Write the number 1 in the largest room.
2. Put an X in F's bedroom.
3. Draw two circles where meals are cooked.
4. Put a circle with a dot inside it in the den.
5. Place three Y's in the master bedroom.
6. Draw a circle around the word <u>Bath</u> that is closest to the master bedroom.
7. Draw a tree outside M's bedroom.
8. Put a pool behind the garage and write the word <u>Pool</u> inside the drawing.
9. Draw three flowers by the front door.
10. Draw a wagon near the two trees.
11. Place an upside-down T in M's bedroom.
12. Draw two squiggly lines in the living room.

COMPREHENSION   F. Can Follow Printed Directions

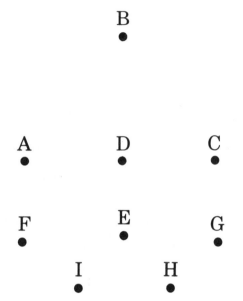

DIRECTIONS:
1. Draw a line from B to D.
2. Draw a line from D to C.
3. Draw a line from C to B.
4. Draw a line from B to A and from A to D.
5. Connect D to E with a short straight line.
6. Connect F to G going through E.
7. Make a swinging line from F to I to H to G.

Happy Sailing!

COMPREHENSION   F. Can Follow Printed Directions

DIRECTIONS: Read sentence <u>a</u> and follow the directions in sentence <u>b</u>.

1. a. The television set needs to be repaired.
   b. Draw a box around the words that tells what needs repairing.

2. a. March 21 is the first day of spring.
   b. Draw a circle around the word meaning a season.

3. a. George went to the drugstore for an ice cream soda.
   b. Underline the word that tells where George went.

4. a. Henriette spent two hours at the dentist's office.
   b. Draw a squiggly line under the word that is a number.

5. a. Polishing shoes is a job few people enjoy.
   b. Draw a picture of what is polished in this sentence.

6. a. Hot soup and a salad taste extra good on a cold day.
   b. Draw an X through the word meaning the opposite of cold.

7. a. The trucks were out spreading sand on the icy highways.
   b. Draw two lines under a word meaning the same as streets.

8. a. The moonlight made the night very bright.
   b. Draw a circle around each of the three words that rhyme.

9. a. The tall building had high ceilings.
   b. Draw an X through the words that have similar meanings.

10. a. The tall tale was about a dog with a short tail.
    b. Draw a box around the words that sound alike.

11. a. Amy had a tomato and lettuce sandwich for lunch.
    b. Draw two lines under the word for a meal.

12. a. Margo sat for hours watching the silver colored grasshopper.
    b. Draw two squiggles under the color word.

COMPREHENSION   G. Can Read for a Definite Purpose

DIRECTIONS: Read each paragraph and write whether a person would read the paragraph for <u>pleasure</u> or to obtain an <u>answer</u> to a question.

1. To be sure that you can get a good picture with your camera, the lens must be clean. It is possible to clean the camera lens by first blowing off the dust and then moistening and wiping gently with a soft tissue.

_____

2. Miss Sue Allen's Parfumerie is located on the corner of Royal and Orleans Street. The shop specializes in fine perfumes. A perfumer is available to blend a unique fragrance for you if this is your desire.

_____

3. The two boys looked at the giant bear's footprint. They had been warned not to wander this far from camp. Soon it would be dark.

_____

4. In 1955, Disneyland opened and it was a dream come true for Walt Disney. He had had a vision of creating a place where families and people from all walks of life could have fun together.

_____

5. As Marc lay under the palm tree, he thought of what it would be like to be a hippopotamus. Would it make a boy feel big and strong? Or would it hurt? Would walking through the jungle hurt his toes?

_____

6. The mountaintop was beautiful. The snow was clean and shone like crystals. Just a few more hours and the climbers would set their flag on the very top of Crazy Mule Mountain. It was a dream come true.

_____

7. When you are taking a picture, stand so that the light falling on the subject comes from behind you or from the side. Keep the scenes clean and simple for a clear picture.

_____

8. The little train knew he could get the lions, elephants, tigers, dogs, and tents to the next town. He just needed a chance. Would the engine man select him?

_____

COMPREHENSION   G. Can Read for a Definite Purpose

DIRECTIONS: Books are read for different purposes. Given below are two reasons for reading. Read the titles of the books that are listed and write the letter for the most common purpose of reading the book.

a. For pleasure
b. To obtain an answer to a question

_____ 1. The Bathtub Mystery

_____ 2. Soccer Rule Book

_____ 3. The Ear and How It Hears

_____ 4. Super Heroes

_____ 5. Olympic Champions 1980

_____ 6. The Muppets in Bear Country

_____ 7. The Discovery of Fuel

_____ 8. Herbie and the Talking Pineapple

_____ 9. Ticket Directory to Disney World

_____ 10. Inside Information on Energy-Saving

_____ 11. The Mad, Mad Cock-A-Doo

_____ 12. Bicycle Tips

COMPREHENSION   G. Can Read for a Definite Purpose

DIRECTIONS: People read for many different reasons. Below are three purposes for reading and a list of things that people read. Decide why a person would probably read each item and write the letter for that purpose in the blank.

a. For pleasure
b. To obtain an answer to a question
c. To obtain a general idea of the content

_____ 1. Train timetable

_____ 2. Menu

_____ 3. Mystery book

_____ 4. TV guide

_____ 5. Directions on a medicine bottle

_____ 6. Back of a cereal box

_____ 7. Comic strip in the newspaper

_____ 8. Directions on a cake mix

_____ 9. Front page of the newspaper

_____ 10. Road map

_____ 11. Letter from Grandpa

_____ 12. Science textbook

_____ 13. Magazine index

_____ 14. Encyclopedia

_____ 15. Sports page of the newspaper

COMPREHENSION   G. Can Read for a Definite Purpose

DIRECTIONS: You are "Super Sleuth" watching a group of people. Each person picks up something and reads it. You are to determine why the person is probably reading the document. Use the three purposes below and place the letter in front of each case.

    a. For pleasure
    b. To obtain an answer to a question
    c. To obtain a general idea of the content

_____ Case 1. A man dashes into a phone booth and picks up the telephone directory.

_____ Case 2. A woman flips through the pages of her address book at the scene of an accident.

_____ Case 3. Tom sits in the library with an encyclopedia in front of him and has a paper and pencil in hand.

_____ Case 4. A man at a magazine stand picks up some magazines and flips through the pages.

_____ Case 5. A teenage boy sits on a park bench reading a Hardy Boys mystery.

_____ Case 6. Mother reads a recipe on how to bake macaroons.

_____ Case 7. A tall, dark man reads the Sports Illustrated magazine.

_____ Case 8. A young woman sits in a car along Highway 20, studying highway maps.

_____ Case 9. Grandma Smith reads a birthday card.

_____ Case 10. A young boy reads a manual called "How to Care for Guppies."

_____ Case 11. Student in library flips through the pages of several books, stopping only at the Table of Contents.

_____ Case 12. Maria looks over the magazines at a magazine counter.

COMPREHENSION   **G. Can Read for a Definite Purpose**

DIRECTIONS: You are given several assignments and each assignment requires you to read. Select from the list below the reasons why you might be reading and mark the letter for the most likely purpose in the blank before each assignment.

    a. To obtain a general idea of the content
    b. For pleasure
    c. To obtain an answer to a question

_____ 1. You want to find the meaning of the word <u>museum</u>.

_____ 2. It's Sunday morning and you are reading the comic section.

_____ 3. You are in the library looking for a book to take on a vacation with you. You are having trouble making a selection, so you look at several books.

_____ 4. Your homework consists of answering five health questions.

_____ 5. The new Sears Roebuck catalog has just arrived and you want to know the price of hunting boots.

_____ 6. You are sitting in the doctor's office and you flip through the pages of several magazines.

_____ 7. You want to know the price of pork chops in the Good Way Grocery Store ad.

_____ 8. Your hobby is skiing and for your birthday you receive a book on <u>Ways to Improve Your Skiing</u>.

_____ 9. You receive a party invitation.

_____ 10. Your science teacher wants you to write a report on why birds fly south in the winter.

_____ 11. Your brother asks you to tell him the hockey scores.

_____ 12. Your sister wins an honor and her picture is in the paper.

COMPREHENSION **G. Can Read for a Definite Purpose**

DIRECTIONS: Read each paragraph and write whether it would usually be read for <u>pleasure</u> or to obtain an <u>answer</u> to a question.

1. The airport is located in a sea of red sand and scrubby bushes. It can handle jumbo jets because the runway is 12,540 feet long. The jets land frequently at this airport on their way to Dubayo.

_____

2. The pig pushed against the door with his snout and walked into the house. Otto the pig came in every night at this time. He walked across the kitchen and into the den. Otto lay down on his own carpet just a few feet from the fireplace.

_____

3. Chris and Greg raked and bagged the leaves. They had been working for several hours. The boys were beginning to get tired. They knew they had to finish the job before they could go to the rodeo.

_____

4. Ed walked into the living room. "It's time for dinner," he said. "Mother wants you to come to the table." The phone rang.

_____

5. Big Molly is a good-looking, fat, sleek hog. She lives with her hog pals in pen No. 777, Hog House 301, at Ashley Farm on Pork Chop Road.

_____

6. There will be two turkey hunting seasons this year. The first season opens March 22 and will close April 2. The second season opens April 4 and will run through April 17. Hunters may bag one turkey a day, two a season, and three for the license period.

_____

7. The group had lunch at Grandma's house. Grandma had made a big pot of old-fashioned vegetable soup, a fruit salad, and brownies for her grandchildren. Grandma enjoyed cooking for a crowd.

_____

8. Put piece Y into log X at the point marked with a 0. Screw bolt T into M at N marked with a +.

_____

COMPREHENSION   **G. Can Read for a Definite Purpose**

DIRECTIONS: Read each sentence and underline the word or words that tell you what a person is doing to or with the book, magazine, or paper. Next, give the correct letter for the purpose of using the reading material.

    a. To obtain an answer to a question
    b. To obtain a general idea of the content
    c. For pleasure

1. Willis is glancing at the Table of Contents of several books at the library.

   Purpose: _____

2. As he drove down the street, Dad read the street signs.

   Purpose: _____

3. Mother searched for the paragraph on how to remove grass stains from John's jeans.

   Purpose: _____

4. Timothy was bored, so he flipped through the pages of the morning paper.

   Purpose: _____

5. Mike was writing a report on Arabian horses and he was using the encyclopedia as a reference.

   Purpose: _____

6. The girls sat on the porch and laughed as they read the comic books.

   Purpose: _____

7. Frank studied the washing directions sewed inside his new jacket.

   Purpose: _____

8. Jonathan read the TV screen at the airport and rushed to Gate D.

   Purpose: _____

COMPREHENSION   G. Can Read for a Definite Purpose

DIRECTIONS: Super Sleuth is visiting a classroom. Super Sleuth listens as the teacher gives directions, asks questions, and teaches. Super Sleuth's job is to decide what the teacher's purposes or reasons are. At the beginning of each statement or question, write the letter of the most likely purpose for reading.

a. To gather information
b. For pleasure
c. To answer a question
d. To get a general idea

_____ 1. Who wrote the story "Mickey and the Giant"?

_____ 2. For the next twenty minutes, you may read any story you wish.

_____ 3. On page 103, find a word that means the same as braid.

_____ 4. Look at the Table of Contents and tell me if this is a health, spelling, or history book.

_____ 5. Before you write your report, read pages 99 and 100 on caring for your teeth.

_____ 6. Look at the third paragraph and tell me what word has the opposite meaning of hard.

_____ 7. Where does the story "Big Thunder" take place?

_____ 8. Look over the story and find three things that tell about Cucko-o-o.

_____ 9. Where did Big John get his bow and arrow?

_____ 10. Pick any story you wish to read during your free time.

COMPREHENSION   G. Can Read for a Definite Purpose

DIRECTIONS: Read the following questions and statements. In the blank, write why you might read or why you think the question is being asked, using the following answers to help you.

    a. To improve word and reading skills
    b. To gather information
    c. To answer a question
    d. For pleasure

1. Which tree is green all year? _____

2. Find the words on this page that sound alike but have different meanings. _____

3. Who put pepper in the witch's stew? _____

4. What story have you read this week that made you smile? _____

5. Find at least five ways to catch a seal by reading the chapter on seals in your science book. _____

6. Where did the story "The Magic Flute" take place? _____

7. Who is this story about? _____

8. Tomorrow, you are to tell the class which book you would like to read again because you enjoyed it so very much. _____

9. List on your paper ten compound words found in this story. _____

10. When does the story "Merrimac" take place? _____

11. Look through the newspaper and cut out all articles on fuel conservation. _____

12. Select a book from the class library and find ten words ending in est. _____

COMPREHENSION   **G. Can Read for a Definite Purpose**

DIRECTIONS: Malcolm has several things he wishes to do this weekend. What is the reason he would be reading as he does the following things? Write <u>for facts</u> or <u>for pleasure</u> after each activity.

1. Reads the directions as he puts together a miniature car.

   _____

2. Finishes reading the book on football heroes.

   _____

3. Bakes a cake for his mother's birthday. _____

4. Reads the Saturday paper. _____

5. Polishes his bicycle with a new kind of polish.

   _____

6. Does his science homework. _____

7. Reads a letter from his Alaskan pen pal. _____

8. Checks on the rules for playing kickball. _____

9. Reads the menu at the Super Heroes Snack Bar.

   _____

10. Looks through the want ads for a used skateboard.

    _____

11. Looks up his uncle's telephone number. _____

12. Reads a magazine on his hobby of stamp collecting.

    _____

COMPREHENSION   H. Can Classify Items

DIRECTIONS: Match each item in Column A with a word in Column B by placing a letter in front of the number in Column A.

<table>
<tr><td colspan="2">Column A</td><td>Column B</td></tr>
<tr><td>_____</td><td>1. June</td><td>a. vegetable</td></tr>
<tr><td>_____</td><td>2. guitar</td><td>b. flower</td></tr>
<tr><td>_____</td><td>3. cabbage</td><td>c. month</td></tr>
<tr><td>_____</td><td>4. hamburger</td><td>d. musical instrument</td></tr>
<tr><td>_____</td><td>5. rocker</td><td>e. dessert</td></tr>
<tr><td>_____</td><td>6. tulip</td><td>f. animal</td></tr>
<tr><td>_____</td><td>7. winter</td><td>g. season</td></tr>
<tr><td>_____</td><td>8. trout</td><td>h. meat</td></tr>
<tr><td>_____</td><td>9. coconut pie</td><td>i. fruit</td></tr>
<tr><td>_____</td><td>10. Password</td><td>j. fish</td></tr>
<tr><td>_____</td><td>11. deer</td><td>k. game</td></tr>
<tr><td>_____</td><td>12. orange</td><td>l. chair</td></tr>
</table>

COMPREHENSION   H. Can Classify Items

DIRECTIONS: Read each sentence. Decide which one of the three topics it belongs to and write the letter of the topic on the line.

Topics
a. Television
b. Camping
c. Playing ball

_____ 1. The cameras were all pointed at the President.

_____ 2. The site was near a lake and under some pine trees.

_____ 3. The director gave instructions to the musicians.

_____ 4. The boys took up sides.

_____ 5. The smell of bacon and coffee awakened them.

_____ 6. The ball was kicked over the goal posts.

_____ 7. The stars twinkled in the sky as we sat around the fire.

_____ 8. The pebbles along the lake were white and smooth.

_____ 9. The score at half time was 10-12.

_____ 10. The sportscaster clipped the microphone to his jacket at seven o'clock sharp.

COMPREHENSION   H. Can Classify Items

DIRECTIONS: In each row, cross out the item that does not belong.

1. Furniture : chair   bed   table   hat
2. Season   : spring   winter   summer   nice
3. Pet   : angel   dog   rabbit   duck
4. Fruit   : orange   carrot   apple   grape
5. Wood   : house   bench   shirt   floor
6. Building : store   church   chimney   fire station
7. Clothes   : sweater   ring   slacks   shirt
8. Sport   : tennis   swimming   football   reading
9. Woman   : uncle   sister   aunt   mother
10. Flower   : tulip   grass   daisy   rose
11. Color   : red   orange   vine   purple
12. Number   : three   yell   six   eight
13. Direction : toward   left   around   once
14. Action   : kick   jump   need   slide
15. Room   : cover   kitchen   bath   den

COMPREHENSION   H. Can Classify Items

DIRECTIONS: Read each line and cross out the word that does not belong with the others.

1. car   gas   bumper   lights   runway

2. bus   driver   seats   dog   brakes

3. garden   seed   clam   plant   weed

4. fish   flower   worm   pole   reel

5. breakfast   toast   pancakes   tennis   eggs   bacon

6. letter   paper   cry   envelope   stamp   mail

7. food   fish   ice cream   watermelon   better   bread

8. hospital   nurse   dark   doctor   temperature   medicine

9. book   print   read   candle   author   cover

10. country   America   land   desert   butcher   mountains

11. pudding   milk   eggs   beat   cook   family

12. Indian   sausage   chief   squaw   tent   hunt

13. ice   snow   sleet   winter   hot   cold

14. wash   water   soap   jelly   rinse   dry

15. trumpet   instrument   ram   music   blow   sound

COMPREHENSION   H. Can Classify Items

DIRECTIONS: Write these words under the headings where they belong.

northwest   bronco   south   game
cowpuncher   trap   pen   fraction
snare   east   add   lasso
multiply   sum   direction shoot

A. Math Words

_____

_____

_____

_____

B. Map Words

_____

_____

_____

_____

C. Rodeo Words

_____

_____

_____

_____

D. Hunting Words

_____

_____

_____

_____

COMPREHENSION   I. Can Use Index

> **Index**
> Airplanes, 2, 5, 87
> Animals, 84-91
> Bears, 85
> Blue fox, 87
> Canning fish, 24
> Cities and towns, 59-62
> Dog team, 85
> Eskimo dogs, 75
> Eskimos, 35-39, 47, 65, 77
> Fishing, 21-29
> Gold mining, 103-107
> History, 66-69
> Statehood, 70-72
> White fox, 88

DIRECTIONS: Using the index above, find the subjects below and write the page or pages on which each is found.

1. bears   _____   6. statehood   _____

2. fishing   _____   7. gold mining   _____

3. white fox   _____   8. animals   _____

4. dog team   _____   9. history   _____

5. airplanes   _____   10. canning fish _____

III

Name: _____ Date: _____

```
┌─────────────────────────────────┐
│    Index of a Library Book      │
│  Americans arrive, 38           │
│  Chinese in Hawaii, 50          │
│  Church people, American, 42    │
│  Climate, 10                    │
│  Cook, Captain James, 30        │
│  Early people, 28               │
│  Formation of the islands, 22   │
│  Japanese in Hawaii, 58         │
│  Joins United States, 105       │
│  Kings of Hawaii, 62            │
│  Pearl Harbor, 90               │
│  Queens of Hawaii, 72           │
│  Traders, American, 48          │
│  Whalers, American, 53          │
└─────────────────────────────────┘
```

DIRECTIONS: Answer each question by writing in the blank following it the number of the page on which you might find the answer.

1. When did Captain Cook visit Hawaii? _____

2. Who was the Hawaiian queen who reigned the longest? _____

3. Who were the first Americans to go to Hawaii? _____

4. What part did the Japanese play in Hawaii's history? _____

5. What happened at Pearl Harbor? _____

6. How were the islands formed? _____

7. What role did the Chinese play in Hawaii's history? _____

8. Why did American traders visit Hawaii? _____

9. When did Hawaii become a state? _____

10. Which king played the most important role in warfare? _____

11. Why were American whalers interested in Hawaii? _____

12. What is Hawaii's climate like? _____

III

COMPREHENSION   I. Can Use Index

Grammar Book Index

Abbreviations, 33, 34, 35
Alphabetical order, 122, 124
Antonyms, 152, 155
Capital letters:
    first word in every line of poem, 41
    in days of the week, 43
    in names of persons, 42
    to begin sentences, 39
Contractions, 55, 56, 58, 59
Games, 121, 123, 135
Letters, 75, 80, 81, 82, 84
Periods:
    after abbreviations, 33
    at end of sentence, 91
Question marks, 100, 101
Reading aloud, 60-65
Reports, 270, 271, 274
Sentences, 60, 61, 62, 63, 64
Speaking clearly, 75, 170, 176
Synonyms, 150, 154, 160
Telephoning, 21, 36, 92
Verbs:
    action words, 147, 227, 247, 257, 268
    definition, 140

DIRECTIONS: Using the index, write on the blank the numbers of the pages on which you would find each of the following topics.

1. Games   _____

2. Telephoning   _____

3. Alphabetical order   _____

4. Periods at the ends of sentences   _____

5. Synonyms   _____

6. Definition of verbs   _____

7. Reading aloud   _____

8. Speaking clearly   _____

9. Abbreviations   _____

10. Sentences   _____

11. Question marks   _____

12. Antonyms   _____

COMPREHENSION   I. Can Use Index

```
                    Index
        Alamo, 250
        American flag, 258-264
        American Fur Company, 253
        Arabs, 61, 83
        Boston Tea Party, 190, 193, 197
        Buffalo, 94-97
        Cattle, 101, 103, 108
        Churches, 10, 14, 18, 29
        Education, 35, 36, 40
        England, 163, 165, 168-170
        Florida, 215-220
        Georgia, 185-189
        Grain, 9, 12, 19, 21
        Great ideas, 184, 258, 301
        Houses and shelter, 51, 100, 109
        Hunting and hunters, 205-206, 218
```

DIRECTIONS: Using the index, answer the following questions by writing the numbers of the pages where the information could be found.

1. Where is Buffalo? _____

2. What is the climate of Georgia? _____

3. What did the hunters use to kill the animals? _____

4. Who was the hero of the Alamo? _____

5. How did the people of England come to America? _____

6. Who went to the Boston Tea Party? _____

7. Who built the first churches? _____

8. How did the Indians harvest grain? _____

9. What are some of the world's great ideas? _____

10. Who began the American Fur Company? _____

11. Tell the story of the American flag. _____

12. Which part of the country raises the most cattle? _____

III   **213**

COMPREHENSION   **I. Can Use Index**

Index

Berries, 24, 35
Deer, 84, 85, 87
Earthworm, 14
Grass, 12
Honey, 39
Lizard, 29
Mountains, 88, 89, 90
Nest, 41
Prairie dogs, 1, 2, 3, 55
Quail, 34, 35, 49
Rat, 73
Sand, 99, 100, 101
Stone, 61, 64
Tree, 46, 57
Whistle, 105
Wind, 81

DIRECTIONS: Using the index, write the numbers of the pages where you would find these subjects.

1. quail _____   8. wind _____

2. grass _____   9. earthworm _____

3. lizard _____   10. mountains _____

4. whistle _____   11. tree _____

5. berries _____   12. prairie dogs _____

6. honey _____   13. rat _____

7. nest _____   14. sand _____

COMPREHENSION   **J. Can Alphabetize Words by First Two Letters**

DIRECTIONS: Number the words in each set in alphabetical order.

A. ____ add
____ any
____ arm
____ apple
____ ax

B. ____ crab
____ clever
____ cap
____ color
____ cheese

C. ____ glue
____ guitar
____ game
____ goat
____ ghost

D. ____ mom
____ mail
____ miss
____ music
____ meat

E. ____ smell
____ stay
____ snow
____ spot
____ salt

F. ____ orange
____ office
____ one
____ own
____ open

G. ____ yule
____ yes
____ you
____ yield
____ yard

H. ____ rooster
____ rub
____ red
____ raisin
____ river

I. ____ pier
____ page
____ prince
____ peanut
____ plow

J. ____ top
____ tap
____ train
____ tunnel
____ three

K. ____ vote
____ vase
____ vine
____ vying
____ vest

L. ____ duck
____ den
____ dragon
____ did
____ dark

COMPREHENSION   **J. Can Alphabetize Words by First Two Letters**

DIRECTIONS: Write the following words in alphabetical order.

cream	awake	school
laugh	coin	match
arctic	lump	bottom
speech	squirrel	phone
pour	barrel	moose
fact	syrup	fiction
strong	paw	

1. _____

2. _____

3. _____

4. _____

5. _____

6. _____

7. _____

8. _____

9. _____

10. _____

11. _____

12. _____

13. _____

14. _____

15. _____

16. _____

17. _____

18. _____

19. _____

20. _____

COMPREHENSION   **J. Can Alphabetize Words by First Two Letters**

DIRECTIONS: Put these names in alphabetical order by last names.

Robert Jones   Mary Broome   Clara Moss
Judy Jasper   Vance Bowen   Mae Lang
Blake Gann   Shirley White   Paul Case
Ed Myers   Jon Clark   Pete Hogan
Terry Lee   Jack Hartnett   Phena Fox
Sandra Kent   Mary Gibbs   Bobby Knight
Sue Wade   Wilfred French

1. _____   11. _____
2. _____   12. _____
3. _____   13. _____
4. _____   14. _____
5. _____   15. _____
6. _____   16. _____
7. _____   17. _____
8. _____   18. _____
9. _____   19. _____
10. _____   20. _____

COMPREHENSION   **J. Can Alphabetize Words by First Two Letters**

DIRECTIONS: Number the words in each set in alphabetical order.

A. _____ around

_____ worm

_____ alligator

_____ clothes

_____ cellar

_____ warm

B. _____ diamond

_____ police

_____ sergeant

_____ dough

_____ propeller

_____ straw

C. _____ toll

_____ control

_____ potato

_____ turkey

_____ cushion

_____ promise

D. _____ guide

_____ minister

_____ helicopter

_____ history

_____ glance

_____ moment

E. _____ explorer

_____ records

_____ forecast

_____ rubber

_____ empty

_____ fearless

F. _____ partner

_____ twigs

_____ turtle

_____ swooped

_____ poked

_____ sergeant

G. _____ puddle

_____ information

_____ parrots

_____ imagine

_____ salt

_____ squaw

H. _____ tepee

_____ crocodiles

_____ stomach

_____ toll

_____ commas

_____ shiver

I. _____ navel

_____ ghost

_____ wilted

_____ guinea

_____ woe

_____ nerves

COMPREHENSION   **J. Can Alphabetize Words by First Two Letters**

DIRECTIONS: Number the words in each set in alphabetical order.

A. ____ reptile   **B.** ____ scales   **C.** ____ wildcat

____ roast   ____ show   ____ wrong

____ rustle   ____ saddle   ____ whisper

____ ripple   ____ snack   ____ waterfall

____ rattle   ____ spatter   ____ woof

D. ____ zig-zag   **E.** ____ twenty   **F.** ____ pork

____ yellow   ____ tack   ____ plop

____ zoo   ____ trout   ____ purr

____ yarn   ____ time   ____ papa

____ yum   ____ too   ____ prickle

G. ____ hopscotch   **H.** ____ kangaroo   **I.** ____ fear

____ hamster   ____ koala   ____ fork

____ hiss   ____ knuckles   ____ fair

____ hull   ____ key   ____ flip

____ herd   ____ king   ____ fish

J. ____ meadow   **K.** ____ doe   **L.** ____ biscuit

____ maple   ____ drip   ____ bell

____ minnow   ____ duchess   ____ by

____ movie   ____ dirt   ____ brown

____ mud   ____ dare   ____ banana

COMPREHENSION   K. Knows Technique of Skimming

DIRECTIONS: Skim the TV schedule below and answer the questions that follow it. You will be timed, so do not read the entire schedule. Skim it.

Time	Channel	Program
7:00	8	Today Show
	4	Good Morning America
	3	Coffee with Sam
8:00	8	Romper Room
	4	Password
	3	Cartoons
8:30	8	Captain Hooligan
9:00	8	Pat and Mike
	4	The Lone Cowboy
	3	Bart and the Circus
10:00	8	The Mountaineers
	4	News
	3	Journey to the Moon

1. What time does the program "The Mountaineers" begin? _____

2. What channel has the "Pat and Mike" program? _____

3. What channel has cartoons? _____

4. What time does "Good Morning America" begin? _____

5. What program does channel 4 feature at 9:00? _____

6. What program begins at 10:00 on channel 3? _____

7. How long is the program "Bart and the Circus"? _____

8. Which channel features the "Today Show"? _____

9. Which channel has news at 10:00? _____

10. What time does "Coffee with Sam" begin? _____

COMPREHENSION   K. Knows Technique of Skimming

DIRECTIONS: Skim the Table of Contents and answer the questions which follow it. You will be given limited time, so remember to skim.

Table of Contents

National News 21
International Affairs 35
Local News 41
Business 48
Justice 55
Science 58
Television 61
Movies 62
Books 64
Religion 68
Education 80
Music 82
Newsmakers 91

1. On what page does the section on Education begin? _____

2. What comes before the Justice section? _____

3. Which section follows Television? _____

4. On what page does the Music section end? _____

5. What comes before the Local News section? _____

6. Which section begins on page 64? _____

7. If you wanted information on churches, to which section would you turn? _____

8. Which section ends on page 34? _____

9. Which section begins on page 91? _____

COMPREHENSION   K. Knows Technique of Skimming

DIRECTIONS: Skim the story below. Next, read the sentences and write True or False in front of each statement. You will be given limited time, so remember to skim the story.

The Chickadee

The chickadee is a small bird. This bird's name and call are very much alike: "Chick-a-dee-dee-dee." A full-grown chickadee seldom weighs more than half an ounce. Though very tiny, it has a heart that beats close to 500 times a minute. The heart beats so fast it sounds like a buzz when heard through a stethoscope.

On cold days, the chickadee has to eat its weight in food. It eats some seeds and small fruits, but the chickadee prefers to eat insects and their eggs. This bird is friendly as well as curious. The chickadee has been known to alight on the head, shoulder, or hand of a person who is quietly watching it. The chickadee fluffs its feathers to keep warm.

The chickadee builds its nest in a hole in a tree or stump. It uses moss, rabbit fur, cow hair, and feathers to make a soft, snug nest.

_____ 1. The chickadee is a large bird.

_____ 2. The chickadee's nest is made in a box.

_____ 3. The chickadee's heart beats very fast.

_____ 4. The name and the call of the bird are very much alike.

_____ 5. The chickadee is afraid of people.

_____ 6. The chickadee uses moss, rabbit fur, and feathers to make a nest.

_____ 7. The chickadee fluffs its feathers in hot weather.

_____ 8. The chickadee likes people.

COMPREHENSION   K. Knows Technique of Skimming

DIRECTIONS: Skim the story and answer the questions that follow.

The Prairie Dog

The prairie dog is not a dog but a rodent. A rodent is an animal with sharp teeth whose teeth continue to grow as their points are worn away by gnawing. Rats, mice, squirrels, and beavers are also rodents. A prairie dog is called "dog" because its danger signal sounds like the bark of a tiny dog.

A prairie dog is about 16 inches long, with tiny ears, shining black eyes, and a short tail. Its body is covered with dull brown fur.

A prairie dog's home is in a hole or a tunnel on a plain, usually in a desert-like place. Groups of prairie dogs live together in villages.

A prairie dog goes into its home when danger is near or when it wants to nap. It spends much time hunting roots and grass and acting as a guard for the village. When an enemy comes near, a guard gives a shrill warning bark. When the signal is given, all prairie dogs stop in their tracks. If the guard does not bark again, they go about their business. If the guard barks a second time, they hurry to their burrows for safety.

1. What kind of home does a prairie dog have? _____

2. What is a rodent? _____

3. How long is a prairie dog? _____

4. Describe the prairie dog's danger signal. _____

5. For what purposes does a prairie dog use its home? _____

_____

Write True or False:

6. _____ Prairie dogs act like guards for one another.

7. _____ Prairie dogs live alone.

8. _____ A prairie dog looks like a dog.

9. _____ This story said that a prairie dog eats snakes and owls.

10. _____ Prairie dogs live in desert-like places.

COMPREHENSION   K. Knows Technique of Skimming

Coventry Klippers Hockey—Home Games—Civil Center			
January	5	Richfly Aces	7:00 PM
	6	West Choctaws	7:00 PM
	15	Rankin Reds	7:00 PM
	19	Broom Blades	7:30 PM
	24	West Choctaws	7:30 PM
	27	Rankin Reds	8:00 PM
	31	Broom Blades	3:00 PM
February	4	Richfly Aces	3:00 PM
	6	Rankin Reds	7:00 PM
	11	Broom Blades	7:30 PM
	16	Bishop Kings	7:30 PM
	20	Bishop Kings	7:30 PM
	22	Richfly Aces	8:00 PM
	28	Rankin Reds	3:00 PM
March	2	Broom Blades	3:00 PM
	3	Bishop Kings	8:00 PM
	5	West Choctaws	7:00 PM
	8	West Choctaws	7:00 PM
	9	Bishop Kings	7:00 PM
	28	Bishop Kings	7:30 PM

For further information and tickets, dial 355-6528.

DIRECTIONS: Skim the schedule and answer the questions in the time allowed by your teacher. Then go back and check your answers.

True or False:

_____ 1. All of the games begin at the same time.
_____ 2. March has the least number of games scheduled.
_____ 3. The last team the Klippers play is West Choctaws.
_____ 4. On February 11, the hockey team will play the Broom Blades at 3:00 PM.
_____ 5. The Richfly Aces are on the January and February Schedules.
_____ 6. The games are played at four different times.

7. What number can you call to order tickets? _____

8. Who will the Klippers play in the second game in February?

_____

9. What time is the game on January 27? _____

10. Who will the Klippers play at the end of March? _____

COMPREHENSION   **L. Can Determine Source to Obtain Information**

DIRECTIONS: Where would you find the answers to the following questions? Select the best source for the information and write the correct letter in the blank.

a. Dictionary   d. Table of Contents
b. Encyclopedia   e. Index
c. Today's newspaper   f. Almanac

_____ 1. Who won the Junior League baseball game yesterday?

_____ 2. What is the meaning of the word coupler?

_____ 3. What time is low tide tomorrow?

_____ 4. How many chapters are there in the book The Story of Trains?

_____ 5. What are the eating habits of sea gulls?

_____ 6. Who won four gold medals at the Summer Olympics in Montreal?

_____ 7. Where is the information on the Prince of Essex in your history book?

_____ 8. Who won the Super Bowl in 1975?

_____ 9. Which syllable is accented in the word triangle?

_____ 10. How many pages are there in your arithmetic book?

_____ 11. When was the first railroad built?

_____ 12. Where in the science book is the information on coral rock?

COMPREHENSION   L. Can Determine Source to Obtain Information

DIRECTIONS: Select the best source of information for the following questions. Write the letter in the blank provided.

a. Almanac   d. Telephone directory
b. Road map   e. Glossary—science book
c. TV guide   f. Index—science book

_____ 1. What is the distance between Orlando and Miami?

_____ 2. Who will be the guest star on "Vampire" Tuesday night?

_____ 3. What is George Adams's address?

_____ 4. What is the definition of photosynthesis?

_____ 5. When was Lyndon Johnson President?

_____ 6. What station features old movies on Sunday mornings at 11:00?

_____ 7. What is the telephone number for City Hall?

_____ 8. Where can a diagram of the inner ear be found?

_____ 9. Which town is north of Broomall?

_____ 10. Where can you find a list of universities?

_____ 11. Where would you find the definition of transfusion?

_____ 12. Where is the description of Pasteur's experiments?

COMPREHENSION   L. Can Determine Source to Obtain Information

DIRECTIONS: Match the kind of information requested with the best source of information.

Information Requested

_____ 1. Number of syllables in encyclopedia

_____ 2. The name of the movie playing in town

_____ 3. Highway number to travel from Sanford to Clinton

_____ 4. Babe Ruth's hitting record

_____ 5. The countries close to Iran

_____ 6. Time and station of the news show "Today"

_____ 7. The number of chapters in your spelling book

_____ 8. Price of winter underwear

_____ 9. Thomas Jefferson's life story

_____ 10. Meaning of a word in your history book that is new to you

_____ 11. Pages where fractions can be found

_____ 12. Number and address of Simon Cleaners

Source of Information

a. Encyclopedia

b. Table of contents

c. Almanac

d. Today's newspaper

e. Dictionary

f. Glossary of history book

g. Road map

h. Atlas

i. Telephone directory

j. Index of arithmetic book

k. TV guide

l. Catalog

COMPREHENSION   L. Can Determine Source to Obtain Information

DIRECTIONS: Match the request for information with the best source to obtain the information.

I.

Request for

_____ 1. Telephone number for ambulance service

_____ 2. Today's weather forecast

_____ 3. Distance from home to the zoo

_____ 4. Time of program, "African Animals"

_____ 5. Meaning of preservation

_____ 6. Price of ten-speed bicycle

Source of Information

a. Dictionary

b. Catalog

c. TV guide

d. Today's newspaper

e. Road map

f. Telephone directory

II.

_____ 1. How Inca Indians hunt

_____ 2. Name and author of book

_____ 3. Recipe for peanut butter cookies

_____ 4. Page on which chapter 4 begins

_____ 5. Joe Louis's boxing record

_____ 6. Sale price of chicken

a. Table of contents

b. Today's newspaper

c. Almanac

d. Encyclopedia

e. Cookbook

f. Title page

COMPREHENSION   L. Can Determine Source to Obtain Information

DIRECTIONS: Read the question and circle the best source to obtain the information.

1. Where would you look to find a train that leaves at three o'clock for Washington D.C.?

    a. newspaper   b. train schedule   c. TV guide   d. almanac

2. Where would you look to buy a second-hand radio?

    a. almanac   b. dictionary   c. newspaper   d. encyclopedia

3. Where would you find the correct spelling of atrocious?

    a. dictionary   b. almanac   c. encyclopedia   d. table of contents

4. Where would you look to find which chapter tells about Little Turtle?

    a. index   b. glossary   c. title page   d. table of contents

5. Where would you look to find out how many eggs to use in making brownies?

    a. TV guide   b. cookbook   c. almanac   d. dictionary

6. Where would you look to find out the time and station of the golf tournament?

    a. TV guide   b. almanac   c. glossary   d. dictionary

7. Where would you find which syllable in a word is accented?

    a. newspaper   b. encyclopedia   c. dictionary   d. almanac

8. Where would you find how many miles per gallon a Mazda gets?

    a. dictionary   b. encyclopedia   c. table of contents   d. almanac

9. Where would you look to find all of the pages in your reading book that teach synonyms?

    a. title page   b. newspaper   c. index   d. table of contents

10. Where would you look to find the meat specials at the grocery store?

    a. newspaper   b. encyclopedia   c. atlas   d. road map

11. Where would you look to find which highway to take to go to Turtle Farm in Warwick?

    a. newspaper   b. encyclopedia   c. road map   d. almanac

12. Where would you look to find the list of Thomas Edison's inventions?

    a. today's newspaper   b. encyclopedia   c. almanac   d. magazine

COMPREHENSION   M. Can Use Maps and Charts

DIRECTIONS: Study the chart and write in the best answer for each of the following questions.

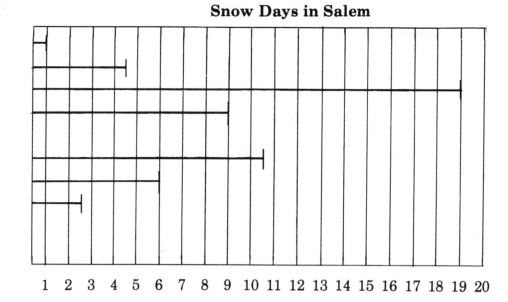

1. Which month had no snow at all? _____

2. Which month had the most snow? _____

3. How many snow days were there in January? _____

4. Which month had 4½ snow days? _____

5. Did October have more or less snow days than November?

_____

6. Which month was best for skiing and sledding?

_____

7. When did the first snow come? _____

8. Do you think it was likely that Salem had snow on the ground at

Christmas? _____

COMPREHENSION   **M. Can Use Maps and Charts**

DIRECTIONS: Study the chart and write the best answer for each question or fill in the missing word in the sentence.

Petting Zoo Animals

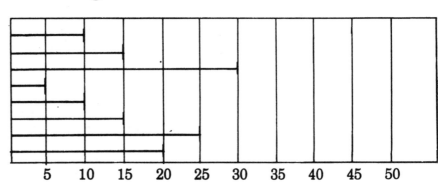

1. How many kinds of animals does the Petting Zoo have?

    _____

2. How many donkeys does the zoo have? _____

3. There are twenty-five _____.

4. Of which animal do they have the fewest? _____

5. Of which animal do they have the most? _____

6. How many pigs are there in the Petting Zoo? _____

7. What do the numbers at the bottom of the chart mean?

    _____

8. Which animal would you like to pet? _____

Name: _____ Date: _____

COMPREHENSION   **M. Can Use Maps and Charts**

DIRECTIONS: Study the chart and write the best answer for each question that follows.

Name of Street

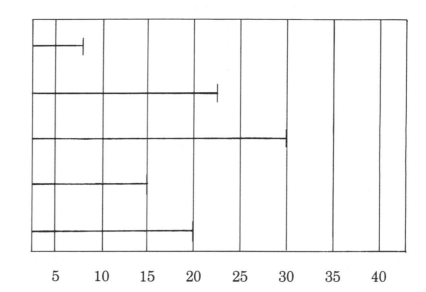

Smith Street

Lincoln Drive

Shady Avenue

Penny Circle

Nickel Avenue

Number of Houses   5   10   15   20   25   30   35   40

1. Which street has the fewest houses? _____

2. What is the largest number of houses on any street? _____

3. What is the name of the street in question 2? _____

4. Which street has twenty houses? _____

5. How many houses are there on Smith Street? _____

6. Which of the two, Penny Circle or Lincoln Drive, has more houses?

   _____

7. What are the numbers at the bottom of the chart?

   _____

8. Does any street have forty houses? _____

COMPREHENSION **M. Can Use Maps and Charts**

DIRECTIONS: Read the statements below the map and do as you are asked. If an answer is required, write it in the blank provided.

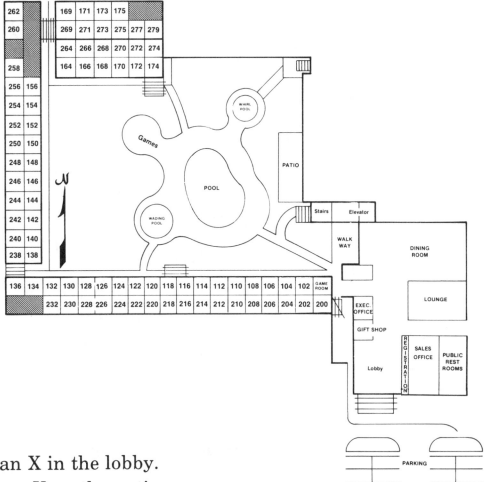

1. Put an X in the lobby.
2. Place a Y on the patio.
3. Draw a line as you walk from the lobby, past the gift shop, and out the door by the executive office. Go to the pool area. Walk around the pool by the whirlpool, the games area, and the wading pool. Then go to room 106.

4. Which rooms are on either side of room 116? _____

5. What is to the left of the sales office? _____

6. What is south of the game section at the pool? _____

7. Put a Z in the dining room.

8. If the car is parked in front of the motel, what direction would you go in to enter the motel?

_____

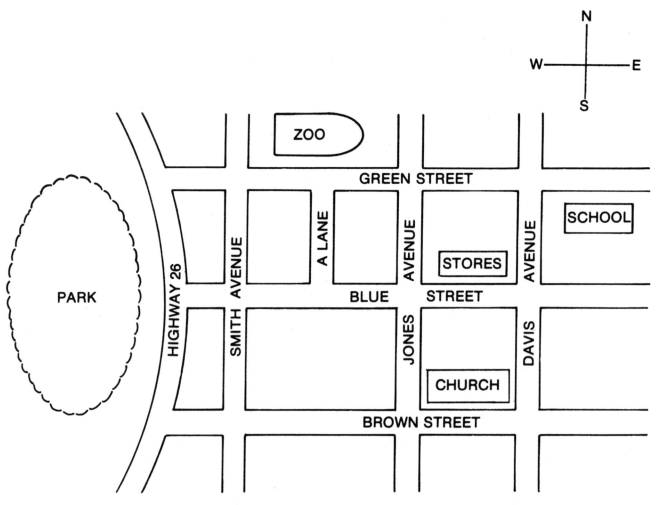

1. Which street is between Green Street and Brown Street?

   _____

2. In which direction does Highway 26 run? _____

3. Does Jones Avenue feed into Highway 26? _____

4. On which corner is the school located? _____

5. Where is the church located? _____

6. On which side of Highway 26 is the park? _____

7. In which direction do the avenues flow? _____

8. How many streets feed into Highway 26? _____

9. In which direction do the streets flow? _____

10. On what street is the Zoo? _____

Answer Key

VOCABULARY

B. Word Meaning   1. a. Function words

Page 24
1. Each	7. than
2. during	8. against
3. Most	9. being
4. more	10. end
5. same	11. thought
6. Should	12. women

Page 25
1. also	7. though
2. enough	8. while
3. men	9. during
4. other	10. through
5. Since	11. enough
6. such	12. while

Page 26
(A)	(B)
1. d	1. e
2. f	2. c
3. e	3. f
4. a	4. b
5. c	5. a
6. b	6. d

Page 27
1. more	7. while
2. other	8. such
3. being	9. during
4. also	10. enough
5. through	11. most
6. than	12. though

Page 28
1. end	7. enough
2. men	8. should
3. against	9. same
4. thought	10. Since
5. during	11. women
6. Each	12. Most

B. Word Meaning   1. b. Direction words

Page 29
1. around	7. toward
2. toward	8. around
3. forward	9. forward
4. backward	10. right
5. right	11. backward
6. left	12. left

Page 30 (A)

(B)

Page 31
1. around	7. backward
2. forward	8. around
3. toward	9. forward
4. left	10. left
5. right	11. toward
6. backward	12. right

Answer Key

B. Word Meaning   1. c. Action words

Page 32
1. g	6. h
2. e	7. c
3. a	8. d
4. i	9. f
5. b	

Page 33
1. carry	7. think
2. kick	8. throw
3. draws	9. travel
4. swim	10. kick
5. skate	11. think
6. push	12. push

Page 34
1. carry	6. swim
2. travel	7. push
3. draw	8. think
4. throw	9. skate
5. kick	10. carry

Page 35
1. travel	7. carry
2. throw	8. kick
3. think	9. skate
4. swim	10. swim
5. push	11. draw
6. draw	12. travel

B. Word Meaning   1. d. Forms of address

Page 36
(A)	1. d	3. b
	2. c	4. a
(B)	1. Mr.	6. Miss (Ms.)
	2. Mrs. (Ms.)	7. Mrs. (Ms.)
	3. Miss (Ms.)	8. Mrs. (Ms.)
	4. Ms.	9. Mr.
	5. Mr.	10. Miss (Ms.)

Page 37
1. Mr.	7. Miss
2. Mrs.	8. Mrs.
3. Miss	9. Mr.
4. Mr.	10. Miss
5. Mrs.	11. Miss
6. Mr.	12. Mr.

Page 38
1. Mr.	7. Mrs.
2. Mrs.	8. Mrs.
3. Mr.	9. Mr.
4. Ms.	10. Miss
5. Mr.	11. Ms.
6. Miss	12. Miss

B. Word Meaning   1. e. Career words

Page 39
1. c	7. f
2. j	8. h
3. g	9. e
4. a	10. d
5. k	11. i
6. b	

Page 40
1. nurse	7. vocation
2. money	8. teacher
3. lawyer	9. training
4. artist	10. operator
5. factory	11. office
6. mechanic	12. money

Page 41
1. h	6. d
2 j	7. b
3. g	8. c
4. a	9. f
5. i	10. e

Page 42
1. artist	9. money
2. lawyer	10. mechanic
3. nurse	11. factory
4. teacher	12. operator
5. artist	13. training
6. vocation	14. office
7. factory	15. training
8. mechanic	

B. Word Meaning   1. f. Color words

Page 43
(A)	1. c	3. d
	2. a	4. b
(B)	1. crackers	5. sand
	2. snow	6. rain
	3. ghost	7. butter
	4. grass	8. vanilla ice cream

Page 44
1. no	7. yes
2. yes	8. no
3. yes	9. yes
4. no	10. no
5. no	11. no
6. no	12. yes

Page 45
(A)	1. no	7. no
	2. no	8. no
	3. yes	9. yes
	4. yes	10. yes
	5. no	11. yes
	6. yes	12. no
(B)	1. purple	7. purple
	2. green	8. brown
	3. green	9. orange
	4. brown	10. brown
	5. orange (yellow)	11. green
	6. purple	12. orange

B. Word Meaning   1. g. Metric words

Page 46
(A)	1. b	3. c
	2. d	4. a
(B)	1. meter	6. liter
	2. liter	7. gram
	3. gram	8. meter
	4. meter	9. gram
	5. centigrade	10. centigrade

Page 47
1. centigrade	6. grams
2. grams	7. centigrade
3. meter	8. meters
4. liter	9. gram
5. liter	10. meters

Page 48
1. liter
2. gram
3. meter
4. liter
5. centigrade
6. gram
7. meter
8. meter
9. centigrade
10. liter
11. meter
12. grams

B. Word Meaning   1. h. Curriculum words

Page 49   Arithmetic
add
less
set
subtract
number
few
odd
even
greater

Science
fall
space
summer
ecology
spring
seasons
winter

History
(Social Studies)
American
country
United States
state
world

Page 50
1. add
2. American
3. country
4. Ecology
5. even
6. fall
7. few
8. greater
9. number
10. less
11. odd
12. seasons

Page 51
1. world
2. winter
3. United States
4. Summer
5. subtract
6. state
7. spring
8. space
9. set
10. greater
11. odd
12. Spring

Page 52
1. number
2. less
3. odd
4. subtract
5. state
6. American
7. country
8. world
9. season
10. winter
11. even
12. few

Page 53
1. add
2. greater
3. ecology
4. fall
5. summer
6. set
7. space
8. spring
9. United States
10. season
11. subtract
12. greater

WORD ANALYSIS
A.   1. Initial consonant sounds

Page 54   A
3t, 6g, 5y, 8d, 10c, 2b, 9n, 1k, 7x, 4m
B
3r, 5v, 7z, 2j, 9l, 1w, 8f, 10p, 6h, 4q

Page 55   Group A
1. v
2. f
3. w
4. b
5. s

Group B
1. c
2. h
3. g
4. z
5. r

Group C
1. v
2. y
3. d
4. m
5. k

Group D
1. p
2. j
3. n
4. y
5. l

Page 56
1. glass glen glow
2. branch bring brook
3. smile smack smug
4. green grove ground
5. friend from fresh

Page 57
1. b
2. c
3. d
4. a
5. f
6. e
7. l
8. g
9. k
10. i
11. h
12. j

Page 58
1. struck
2. christen
3. schedule
4. splint
5. throne, three
6. spree
7. strong
8. Christmas
9. throne
10. school
11. spree
12. splash
13. spring
14. three
15. stream
16. splashed
17. school
18. Christmas

Page 59
1. ch
2. gr
3. m
4. pl
5. th
6. bl
7. sw
8. th
9. sl
10. sp
11. br
12. l
13. c
14. t
15. k
16. str (or spr)
17. w
18. sn (or cl)
19. f
20. r

A.   2. Short and long vowel sounds

Page 60
1. o short
2. i long
3. a short
4. i long
5. a short
6. a short
7. i long
8. i short
9. u short
10. a long
11. u short
12. a long
13. o long
14. u long
15. e short
16. e long
17. o short
18. e short
19. e short
20. o long

Answer Key

Page 61 Part A.

1. get	6. wet
2. until	7. best
3. wag	8. lick
4. shut	9. doll
5. pick	10. neck

Part B.

1. bugle	6. duke
2. cubes	7. tigers
3. cute	8. wild
4. huge	9. cold
5. bee	10. rolled

Page 62

Long—key, like, pole, shape, baked
Short—best, bare, king, bad, clock, inn, thing, bug, mum, trust

Page 63

1. u short	9. a long
2. o short	10. a short
3. a short	11. i long
4. e long	12. o short
5. u short	13. u long
6. e long	14. i short
7. o short	15. e short
8. o long	

Page 64

1. fed	9. due
2. hum	10. fold
3. like	11. hate
4. go	12. so
5. nut	13. lung
6. same	14. pig
7. rice	15. seed
8. pad	

A.   3.a. Adding s, es, d, ed, ing, er, est

Page 65

1. walking	11. traders
2. sweeter	12. carrots
3. shoes	13. tallest
4. rabbits	14. shaped
5. shortest	15. witches
6. singing	16. purring
7. ringing	17. pulled
8. whistled	18. skated
9. Suffixes	19. inches
10. splashed	20. invited

Page 66

1. s	11. ed
2. er	12. es
3. es	13. est
4. er	14. er
5. est	15. d
6. s	16. s
7. ing	17. ing
8. er	18. d
9. es	19. ed
10. ing	20. est

Page 67

1. cats	6. larger
2. fastest	7. exclaimed
3. black	8. Drinking
4. grapes	9. counted
5. leaner	10. reached

11. enjoyed	14. minded
12. ditches	15. painted
13. noted	16. knocking

A.   3.b. Dropping final e and adding ing

Page 68 Part A.

1. chasing	6. sliding
2. waving	7. smoking
3. smiling	8. freezing
4. inviting	9. giving
5. placing	10. becoming

Part B.

1. wiggle	6. behave
2. parade	7. glance
3. bike	8. squeeze
4. choke	9. force
5. whistle	10. hide

Page 69

1. b	9. a
2. a	10. b
3. c	11. a
4. a	12. a
5. b	13. c
6. c	14. b
7. a	15. b
8. b	

A.   3.a. Adding s, es, d, ed, ing, er, est
      b. Dropping final e and adding ing

Page 70

1. excite	9. watch
2. doze	10. dish
3. chatter	11. jump
4. egg	12. head
5. agree	13. expect
6. wobble	14. fast
7. sharp	15. great
8. tall	16. close

Page 71

1. blade	11. mutter
2. roll	12. move
3. piece	13. hibernate
4. answer	14. acorn
5. freeze	15. honk
6. brace	16. proud
7. pinch	17. stitch
8. boat	18. clean
9. soft	19. unite
10. test	20. quick

Page 72

1. leader	11. smartest
2. bravest	12. rushed
3. wishing	13. lifted
4. friends	14. moving
5. shortest	15. roller
6. smoking	16. pocketing
7. sniffed	17. stamped
8. raced	18. voiced
9. fences	19. shined
10. brushes	20. wishes

Page 73

1. adds, added, adding, adder
2. spreads, spreading, spreader
3. vines
4. spells, spelled, spelling, speller

5. sinks, sinking, sinker
6. grander, grandest
7. melts, melted, melting
8. makes, making, maker
9. higher, highest
10. lights, lighted, lighting, lighter, lightest
11. bares, bared, baring, barer, barest
12. blocks, blocked, blocking, blocker
13. calms, calmed, calming, calmer, calmest
14. supposes, supposed, supposing
15. imagines, imagined, imagining
16. books, booked, booking

Page 74
1. kiss
2. need
3. stroke
4. reach
5. tight
6. smart
7. pass
8. tax
9. twist
10. fist
11. nice
12. bend
13. eel
14. puzzle
15. bike
16. weak
17. count
18. dear
19. force
20. warn

A. 3.c. *Doubling the consonant before adding* ing

Page 75
1. wagging
2. grinning
3. slipping
4. thinning
5. sledding
6. rubbing
7. rapping
8. skinning
9. spotting
10. grabbing
11. stripping
12. hopping
13. stopping
14. cutting
15. popping
16. swimming

Page 76
1. fit
2. nod
3. run
4. rip
5. nap
6. strip
7. sit
8. shop
9. shed
10. pen
11. stir
12. can
13. propel
14. chop
15. fan

Page 77
1. fill
2. lick
3. lean
4. get
5. drag
6. warn
7. beg
8. trot
9. pad
10. grab
11. flip
12. win
13. flop
14. bed
15. jut

Page 78
1. begging
2. hemming
3. swimming
4. gumming
5. chumming
6. bogging
7. chugging
8. canning
9. blotting
10. bobbing
11. netting
12. slipping
13. planning
14. spanning
15. slamming

Page 79
1. hemming
2. pinning
3. chugging
4. sitting
5. hugging
6. stripping
7. Bagging
8. ripping
9. chopping
10. clipping
11. skimming
12. slapping
13. wrapping

A. 3.d. *Changing* y *to* i *before adding* es

Page 80
1. cries
2. babies
3. bodies
4. flies
5. fifties
6. countries
7. nineties
8. libraries
9. funnies
10. factories
11. puppies
12. parties
13. dries
14. hurries
15. fries

Page 81
1. pries
2. fries
3. tries
4. flies
5. dries
6. carries
7. studies
8. ponies
9. buggies
10. spies

Page 82
1. pry
2. dry
3. story
4. colony
5. fly
6. worry
7. sky
8. hurry
9. family
10. butterfly
11. carry
12. berry
13. hobby
14. penny
15. twenty

Page 83
1. tries
2. flies
3. stories
4. empties
5. butterflies
6. bunnies
7. pries
8. ponies
9. candies
10. berries
11. counties
12. marries

Page 84
1. posy
2. factory
3. sky
4. memory
5. candy
6. country
7. jelly
8. kitty
9. marry
10. city
11. carry
12. cherry
13. fifty
14. puppy
15. lullaby

A. 3.a,b,c,d. *Changes in words for endings*

Page 85
1. d penn(y)
2. a table
3. a pick
4. b stag(e)
5. b leav(e)
6. a train
7. d lad(y)
8. a old
9. a quiet
10. d sk(y)
11. a close
12. c trap
13. a toll
14. d hurry
15. b rais(e)

Page 86
1. tip
2. start
3. splash
4. shame
5. spread
6. vase
7. talk
8. swim

Answer Key

9. grin
10. taste
11. time
12. jet
13. forty
14. thrash
15. shout
16. spade
17. rug
18. tell
19. sharp
20. hurry

Page 87 Several possible answers are correct. The student only needs to write one new word to be correct unless otherwise directed.
1. blankets, blanketed, blanketing
2. camps, camped, camping, camper
3. drags, dragged, dragging
4. puppies
5. sleds, sledding, sledder
6. jellies, jellied, jellying
7. fries, fried, frying, fryer
8. slims, slimmer, slimmest
9. blazes, blazed, blazer, blazing
10. boils, boiled, boiler, boiling
11. prays, prayed, praying, prayer
12. twenties
13. tapes, taped, taping, taper
14. quits, quitter, quitting
15. tastes, tasted, tasting, taster

Page 88
1. running
2. howled
3. departing
4. working
5. tallest
6. cookies
7. rained
8. carrots
9. enjoys
10. reading
11. leaped
12. blinking

Page 89
1. a
2. a
3. a
4. c
5. a
6. c
7. a
8. a
9. a
10. a
11. b
12. a
13. d
14. b
15. c

A. 4.a. Vowel in one-syllable word is short

Page 90
1. short
2. long
3. short
4. long
5. short
6. short
7. short
8. short
9. long
10. short
11. short
12. short
13. long
14. short
15. short

Page 91 Part A.
1. ham
2. hat
3. nut
4. pet
5. top
6. pig
7. dog
8. pond
9. shop
10. hop

Part B.
1. gas
2. lick, lock, lack, luck
3. map, mop
4. frog

5. run, ran
6. calf
7. bun, Ben, bin, ban
8. sled, slid
9. shell, shall
10. ton, tin, ten, tan
11. stop, step
12. beg, big, bag, bug, bog

A. 4.b. Vowel in syllable or word ending in e is long

Page 92
1. short
2. long
3. short
4. long
5. short
6. long
7. long
8. short
9. long
10. long
11. long
12. long
13. long
14. short
15. long
16. short
17. long
18. short
19. long
20. long

Page 93
1. dime
2. hides
3. bake
4. cape
5. take
6. rake
7 cake
8. gate
9. white
10. Wipe
11. tame
12. late
13. bike
14. June
15. tune

A. 4.a.,b. Short and long vowels

Page 94
1. S
2. L
3. S
4. L
5. L
6. S
7. S
8. S
9. S
10. L
11. L
12. S
13. S
14. L
15. S
16. L
17. S
18. S
19. S
20. L
21. S
22. L
23. L
24. S
25. S
26. L
27. L
28. L
29. S
30. L
31. L
32. L
33. S
34. L
35. L
36. L

A. 4.c. Two vowels together, first is often long and second is silent

Page 95
1. pie
2. paint
3. coat
4. croak
5. meat
6. green
7. tie
8. boat
9. soap
10. blue
11. float
12. feet
13. peas
14. goat
15. seals

240

Page 96
1. roof
4. pause
6. bread
11. head
14. haul
16. stool
18. tooth
20. sauce
25. roar
26. shoot
29. air

Page 97 Part A.
1. re(a)d
2. sa(y)
3. we(a)k
4. whe(a)t
5. te(a)m
6. da(y)
7. sna(i)l
8. na(i)l
9. co(a)st
10. who(a)
11. me(a)t
12. fe(a)st
13. be(e)f
14. ste(a)m
15. be(a)k

B.
1. e
2. j
3. d
4. g
5. b
6. i
7. c
8. f
9. a
10. h

A.   4.d. *Vowel alone in word is short*

Page 98
1. No
2. Yes
3. No
4. Yes
5. Yes
6. No
7. No
8. Yes
9. No
10. No
11. No
12. No
13. No
14. No
15. No
16. No
17. Yes
18. Yes
19. No
20. Yes

Page 99
1. short
2. short
3. long
4. short
5. short
6. long
7. short
8. short
9. short
10. long
11. short
12. short
13. short
14. long
15. short
16. short
17. short
18. long
19. short
20. long
21. long
22. long
23. long
24. short
25. short

A.   4.a,b,c,d. *Review of vowel rules*

Page 100
1. long b
2. short a, d
3. short a, d
4. long b
5. short a, d
6. long b
7. short a, d
8. short a, d
9. short a, d
10. short a, d
11. long b
12. short a, d
13. long b
14. long c
15. short a, d

Page 101
1. hope
2. use
3. dime
4. pin
5. bite
6. at
7. cut
8. hat

9. rod
10. note
11. box
12. bike
13. net
14. pail
15. hid
16. vase
17. tame
18. tune
19. cake
20. gate

Page 102
1. long
2. long
3. long
4. short
5. short
6. short
7. long
8. short
9. long
10. long
11. short
12. long
13. short
14. long
15. short
16. short
17. short
18. short
19. long
20. short

Page 103 Part I.
5a
8b
1c
7d
6e
10f
9g
4h
2i
3j

Part II.
9a
10b
1c
8d
7e
2f
3g
4h
6i
5j

Page 104
1. b
2. b
3. a, d
4. c
5. a, d
6. a, d
7. a, d
8. a, d
9. c
10. c
11. b
12. a, d
13. b, c
14. a, d
15. b

A.   5. *C followed by i, e, y makes s sound*
    C followed by a, o, u makes k sound

Page 105 C = S Sound: cent, city, center, circle, cell
C = K Sound: come, control, customer, caught, case, cold, coin, Cuba, count, coral

Page 106
1. K
2. K
3. S
4. K
5. S
6. K
7. S
8. K
9. K
10. S
11. K
12. K
13. K
14. S
15. K
16. K
17. K
18. S
19. K
20. S

Page 107
1. K
2. K
3. K
4. K
5. K
6. K
7. K
8. K
9. S
10. K
11. K
12. S

Answer Key

13. K	17. K
14. S	18. K
15. K	19. K
16. K	20. K

Page 108

1. S	11. K
2. K	12. K
3. S	13. S
4. S	14. K
5. K	15. K
6. S	16. K
7. S	17. S
8. K	18. S
9. S	19. K
10. K	20. K

Page 109 C = S Sound: acid, juice, pencil, decide, circle, special, place, fence, face, glance, voice, cymbal

C = K Sound: concrete, acorn, contract, cover, canyon, Africa, carve, cave, code, circle, cake, suitcase, because

A. 6. *G followed by* i, e, y *makes* j *sound*
G followed by a, o, u *makes* guh *sound*

Page 110 G = J Sound: ginger, generate, giraffe, giant, gym, gem, gentle

G = Guh Sound: game, goose, got, gut, guitar, gum, gate, guy, good, golden, gang

Page 111

1. guh	11. guh
2. guh	12. j
3. guh	13. j
4. guh	14. guh
5. guh	15. j
6. j	16. guh
7. guh	17. j
8. guh	18. j
9. j	19. guh
10. guh	20. j

Page 112

1. guh	9. guh
2. j	10. guh
3. guh	11. guh
4. guh	12. j
5. j	13. guh
6. guh	14. guh
7. j	15. j
8. j	

Page 113

1. j	11. j
2. j	12. j
3. j	13. guh
4. j	14. j
5. guh	15. j
6. guh	16. guh
7. j	17. guh
8. guh	18. j
9. guh	19. guh
10. j	20. j

Page 114 G = Soft Sound = J: wedge, bulge, engine, general, serge, voyage, urge, judge, genius

G = Hard Sound = Guh: goblin, argument, elegant, mango, goal, gutter, cargo, hogan, gable, gust, guess

A. 7. *Silent letters in* kn, wr, gn

Page 115

1. w	11. g
2. w	12. g
3. k	13. k
4. g	14. w
5. w	15. k
6. g	16. w
7. k	17. g
8. w	18. k
9. k	19. w
10. g	20. k

Page 116

1. kn	9. kn
2. wr	10. wr
3. gn	11. gn
4. kn	12. wr
5. wr	13. gn
6. gn	14. gn
7. kn	15. wr
8. gn	16. kn

Page 117 Part A:

1. know	6. knit
2. knock	7. knew
3. knot	8. knell
4. knob	9. knack
5. knoll	10. knead

Part B:

1. wrap	6. wreck
2. wrack	7. wren
3. wring	8. wrong
4. wrist	9. wry
5. wrath	10. wrote

Page 118

1. knock	9. wren
2. wreck	10. wrist
3. gnarled	11. wrecker
4. knob	12. wreath
5. knee	13. gnome
6. knife	14. gnats
7. knot	15. knit
8. wrap	

Page 119

1. g	11. w
2. w	12. g
3. w	13. k
4. k	14. g
5. w	15. k
6. w	16. w
7. k	17. k
8. w	18. g
9. k	19. k
10. w	20. w

B. 1. *Forming plurals*

Page 120 Part A:

1. puppies	4. knives
2. gloves	5. pretzels
3. taxes	6. tunnels

	7. bottles	9. kisses
	8. twenties	10. halves

Part B:

1. calf	6. bullet
2. mongoose	7. funny
3. guest	8. ranch
4. harness	9. sandwich
5. scarf	10. bunny

Page 121 Part A:

3a	1f
7b	2g
10c	5h
9d	6i
8e	4j

Part B:

6a	4f
3b	5g
9c	1h
2d	10i
7e	8j

Page 122

1. b	9. a
2. a	10. b
3. c	11. b
4. a	12. a
5. b	13. a
6. b	14. b
7. c	15. a
8. a	

Page 123

1. ducks	11. calves
2. babies	12. farms
3. ranches	13. flies
4. wolves	14. inches
5. rags	15. bridges
6. classes	16. bats
7. bowls	17. countries
8. selves	18. raccoons
9. skies	19. loaves
10. lasses	20. ladies

Page 124

1. b	9. c
2. b	10. c
3. b	11. a
4. a	12. c
5. b	13. a
6. a	14. b
7. b	15. c
8. a	

B.   2. Similarities of sound

Page 125

1. k	9. kit
2. lon	10. shun
3. f	11. k
4. e	12. en
5. f	13. k
6. k	14. e
7. k	15. el
8. f	

Page 126 A:

1. d	5. g
2. e	6. h
3. c	7. b
4. f	8. a

B:

1. c	5. g
2. e	6. b
3. h	7. d
4. a	8. f

Page 127

1. b	9. c
2. c	10. b
3. a	11. c
4. a	12. a
5. b	13. b
6. a	14. a
7. b	15. c
8. a	

Page 128 Part A:

1. c	5. d
2. a	6. h
3. f	7. b
4. g	8. e

Part B:

1. e	5. h
2. d	6. b
3. a	7. c
4. g	8. f

Page 129 Part A:

1. b	5. h
2. f	6. c
3. g	7. d
4. a	8. e

Part B:

1. c	5. h
2. a	6. b
3. e	7. d
4. g	8. f

B.   3. Roman numerals I through X

Page 130 Part A:

a. 1	f. 5
b. 4	g. 3
c. 6	h. 9
d. 2	i. 8
e. 10	j. 7

Part B:

a. X	f. II
b. VI	g. IX
c. III	h. IV
d. I	i. VII
e. VIII	j. V

Page 131

1. III	9. VI
2. X	10. VII
3. V	11. I
4. I	12. V
5. II	13. X
6. IX	14. V
7. VIII	15. I
8. IV	

Page 132

1. 8	4. 5
2. 3	5. 10
3. 2	6. 9

Answer Key

7. 7
8. 6
9. 4
10. 1
11. 10

12. 1
13. 5
14. 5
15. 1

Page 133
a. 2
b. 6
c. 10
d. 4
e. 1
f. 5
g. 3
h. 7

i. 10
j. 5
k. 1
l. 8
m. 10
n. 9
o. 5

Page 134 Part A:
a. I
b. VII
c. III
d. IV
e. V

f. X
g. II
h. IX
i. VI
j. VIII

Part B:
1. V
2. II
3. I
4. X
5. V

6. I
7. X
8. V
9. I
10. X

C. 1. *Syllabication: As many syllables in a word as there are vowels*

Page 135
1. 1
2. 2
3. 1
4. 2
5. 2
6. 2
7. 2
8. 1
9. 1
10. 1

11. 2
12. 1
13. 1
14. 2
15. 1
16. 1
17. 2
18. 2
19. 1
20. 2

Page 136
a. 2
b. 1
c. 2
d. 1
e. 1
f. 1
g. 1
h. 2
i. 1
j. 1

k. 1
l. 2
m. 3
n. 1
o. 3
p. 1
q. 2
r. 2
s. 1
t. 2

Page 137 Part A:
a. 2
b. 1
c. 2
d. 2
e. 1
f. 2
g. 2
h. 2
i. 2
j. 2

k. 2
l. 3
m. 3
n. 2
o. 4
p. 2
q. 2
r. 1
s. 3
t. 3

Part B:
a. 2
b. 1
c. 1
d. 3
e. 3
f. 1
g. 2
h. 1
i. 2
j. 1

k. 2
l. 2
m. 2
n. 2
o. 2
p. 1
q. 1
r. 2
s. 2
t. 2

Page 138
1. 3
2. 2
3. 3
4. 1
5. 3
6. 2
7. 2
8. 1
9. 2
10. 1
11. 2
12. 2
13. 2
14. 3
15. 3

16. 2
17. 2
18. 2
19. 2
20. 2
21. 2
22. 3
23. 1
24. 2
25. 2
26. 3
27. 1
28. 2
29. 2
30. 1

Page 139
a. 3
b. 1
c. 2
d. 1
e. 2
f. 2
g. 2
h. 2
i. 2
j. 1

k. 2
l. 2
m. 2
n. 2
o. 2
p. 2
q. 2
r. 3
s. 3
t. 2

C. 2. *Syllabication: Single consonant between two vowels*

Page 140
1. sev/en
2. shov/el
3. me/sa
4. na/vel
5. clos/et
6. re/turn
7. mo/ment
8. cor/al
9. ti/tle
10. Ni/na

11. tu/na
12. vis/it
13. ho/gan
14. sec/ond
15. pa/per
16. mag/ic
17. lo/cate
18. Lo/la
19. la/ter
20. fa/mous

Page 141
1. a
2. a
3. c
4. c
5. b
6. b
7. c
8. b

9. b
10. b
11. c
12. a
13. c
14. b
15. a

Page 142
1. mo/tor
2. pre/tend
3. a/bout

4. fa/vor
5. ho/tel
6. ra/dar

7. a/head
8. ca/ble
9. he/ro
10. li/ter
11. ti/ger
12. no/ble
13. sal/ad
14. lo/cust
15. be/hind
16. ma/son
17. pe/so
18. clo/ver
19. sa/lute
20. stu/pid

Page 143
1. b
2. a
3. a
4. a
5. b
6. a
7. a
8. a
9. b
10. a
11. a
12. b
13. a
14. b
15. a
16. a
17. b
18. a
19. b
20. b

Page 144 Part A:
1. o/pen
2. a/bout
3. bod/y
4. liz/ard
5. e/ven
6. fin/ish
7. co/zy
8. clos/et
9. bea/ver
10. be/low
11. fa/mous
12. i/dea
13. ho/mer
14. Da/vid
15. a/like

Part B:
1. b
2. b
3. a
4. a
5. b
6. a
7. a
8. b
9. a
10. a

C. 3. Syllabication: Double consonant

Page 145
1. bat/tle
2. nib/ble
3. as/sure
4. man/ner
5. shud/der
6. lit/tle
7. of/fer
8. fel/low
9. rob/ber
10. les/son
11. Rod/dy
12. ber/ry
13. ap/pear
14. set/tle
15. sug/gest

Page 146
1. a
2. b
3. b
4. a
5. b
6. a
7. a
8. b
9. a
10. b
11. b
12. a
13. b
14. a
15. a
16. b
17. b
18. a
19. b
20. a

Page 147
1. rat/tle, cat/tle, lit/tle
2. pep/per, dol/lar, let/ter
3. ruf/fle, man/ner, set/tle
4. Sam/my, Nib/ble, Cat/tle
5. com/mon, cat/tle, bat/ter
6. col/lect, sup/pose, bur/row
7. fol/low, spat/ter bal/loons

8. let/ter, let/tuce, lit/ter
9. as/sure, mid/dle, mir/ror
10. sad/dle, nar/row, smell/ing

Page 148
1. drib/ble
2. pup/py
3. lad/der
4. sup/pose
5. bur/row
6. mid/dle
7. sit/ter
8. stir/rup
9. sum/mer
10. sud/den
11. sup/port
12. swal/low
13. val/ley
14. wor/ry
15. yel/low

Page 149
1. Yes
2. No
3. Yes
4. Yes
5. No
6. Yes
7. Yes
8. No
9. Yes
10. Yes
11. No
12. Yes
13. No
14. Yes
15. Yes
16. Yes
17. Yes
18. Yes
19. Yes
20. Yes

D. Hyphenate words using syllable rules

Page 150
1. vel-vet
2. her-ring
3. wed-ding
4. sup-pose
5. wa-ter
6. sol-id
7. tid-al
8. fol-low
9. whir-ring
10. Ju-no
11. rad-ish
12. trot-ted
13. spar-row
14. spo-ken
15. dog-gy

Page 151
1. no
2. no
3. yes
4. yes
5. yes
6. no
7. yes
8. yes
9. yes
10. yes
11. no
12. yes
13. yes
14. yes
15. no
16. yes
17. yes
18. yes
19. yes
20. yes

Page 152
1. A
2. B
3. B
4. A
5. A
6. B
7. A
8. B
9. A–B
10. A
11. A
12. B
13. A
14. A
15. B
16. A
17. A
18. B
19. A
20. B

Page 153
1. word
2. yel-low
3. vis-it
4. val-ley
5. lake
6. sta-tion
7. bot-tle
8. sure
9. pup-py
10. be-gan
11. sud-den
12. po-lice
13. sled
14. pa-rade
15. scis-sors
16. gui-tar

Answer Key

17. mid-dle
18. vi-sa

19. bet-ter
20. wet

Page 154

1. pres-sure
2. fi-nal
3. pup-pet
4. sug-gest
5. de-clare
6. shov-el
7. mit-ten
8. a-way

9. wa-ter
10. of-fer
11. les-son
12. de-cide
13. po-lite
14. trav-el
15. re-port

E. Use of primary accent mark

Page 155

1. Yes
2. Yes
3. No
4. Yes
5. Yes
6. Yes
7. Yes
8. Yes

9. Yes
10. No
11. Yes
12. Yes
13. No
14. Yes
15. Yes

Page 156

1. pu'-pil
2. vow'-el
3. i'-ron
4. Jen'-ny
5. gen'-tle
6. fol'-low
7. heav'-y
8. fuzz'-y

9. cra'-dle
10. cof'-fee
11. flow'-er
12. din'-er
13. cor'-ner
14. hap'-pen
15. dan'-ger

Page 157

1. a
2. b
3. a
4. a
5. a
6. b
7. b
8. a

9. b
10. a
11. a
12. b
13. b
14. b
15. a

Page 158

1. wa'-ter
2. rub'-bing
3. yel'-low
4. sup'-per
5. an'-gry
6. thank'-ful
7. pow'-der
8. re-port'

9. don'-key
10. rab'-bit
11. wag'-on
12. pack'-ing
13. par'-ty
14. our-selves'
15. tad'-pole

Page 159

a. 1
b. 1
c. 1
d. 1
e. 1
f. 1
g. 1

h. 1
i. 1
j. 1
k. 1
l. 1
m. 1
n. 1

o. 1
p. 1
q. 1

r. 1
s. 2
t. 1

F. Accent first syllable unless it is a prefix, otherwise accent second syllable

Page 160

1. <u>yes</u>-ter-day
2. de-<u>mand</u>
3. <u>sto</u>-ry-tell-er
4. mis-<u>take</u>
5. be-<u>came</u>
6. pre-<u>sume</u>
7. <u>con</u>-crete
8. <u>cou</u>-ple
9. <u>tri</u>-cy-cle
10. <u>wood</u>-chuck
11. <u>cow</u>-boy
12. de-<u>part</u>-ment
13. <u>fall</u>-ing
14. <u>sky</u>-scrap-er
15. <u>hum</u>-mer

16. <u>no</u>-bod-y
17. pre-<u>tend</u>
18. sub-<u>mit</u>
19. <u>Nav</u>-a-ho
20. com-<u>mand</u>
21. tre-<u>men</u>-dous
22. <u>fif</u>-ty
23. <u>thank</u>-ful
24. <u>flag</u>-pole
25. be-<u>head</u>-ed
26. <u>pas</u>-sen-ger
27. <u>el</u>-bow
28. in-tro-<u>duce</u>
29. <u>drip</u>-pings
30. <u>flip</u>-per

Page 161

1. Yes
2. No
3. Yes
4. Yes
5. Yes
6. Yes
7. No
8. Yes
9. No
10. Yes

11. Yes
12. No
13. Yes
14. Yes
15. Yes
16. Yes
17. No
18. Yes
19. Yes
20. Yes

Page 162

1. b
2. b
3. a
4. a
5. b
6. a
7. b
8. a

9. a
10. b
11. a
12. b
13. a
14. b
15. a

Page 163

1. in-<u>deed</u>
2. <u>gog</u>-gles
3. <u>no</u>-ble
4. <u>o</u>-cean
5. per-<u>haps</u>
6. <u>hope</u>-less
7. trans-<u>fer</u>
   (or <u>trans</u>-fer)

8. a-<u>bed</u>
9. en-<u>trust</u>
10. dis-<u>cuss</u>
11. in-<u>tact</u>
12. <u>hol</u>-ly
13. in-<u>ten</u>-tion
14. <u>fos</u>-sil
15. dis-<u>arm</u>

Page 164

1. became
2. enjoy
3. before
4. unhappy
5. misread
6. misplaced
7. misunderstood
8. remove

9. moonlight
10. retrace
11. rebuilt
12. pockets
13. refilled
14. untied
15. overhead

COMPREHENSION

A. Can Find Main Idea in Story

Page 165   1. C   4. D
2. A   6. ✓
3. B

Page 166   1. b   4. a
2. a   5. b
3. b

Page 167   A. 3   D. 2
B. 1   E. 2
C. 3

Page 168   1. D   4. C
2. B   5. B
3. A

Page 169   1. a   4. c
2. b   5. a
3. a

B. Can Keep Events in Proper Sequence

Page 170   A. 2, 4, 1, 3   C. 2, 3, 4, 1
B. 2, 4, 3, 1   D. 4, 3, 2, 1

Page 171   A. 2, 1, 3, 4   C. 3, 4, 2, 1
B. 2, 4, 1, 3   D. 2, 4, 1, 3

Page 172   A. 2, 3, 1, 4   B. 4, 2, 1, 3

Page 173   A. 3, 1, 4, 2   F. 4, 2, 1, 3
B. 2, 1, 3, 4   G. 3, 1, 2, 4
C. 4, 2, 1, 3   H. 2, 3, 4, 1
D. 3, 1, 4, 2   I. 3, 1, 4, 2
E. 1, 4, 2, 3   J. 1, 4, 2, 3

Page 174   A. 4, 2, 1, 3   C. 1, 3, 4, 2
B. 2, 3, 4, 1   D. 4, 1, 3, 2

C. Can Draw Logical Conclusions

Page 175   1. a   6. b
2. c   7. b
3. a   8. c
4. c   9. a
5. a   10. c

Page 176   1. a   6. a
2. d   7. c
3. c   8. b
4. b   9. d
5. d   10. c

Page 177   1. c   6. b
2. a   7. c
3. b   8. a
4. b   9. c
5. a   10. c

Page 178   1. a   4. c
2. c   5. b
3. b

Page 179   1. bird   9. milk
2. flowers   10. glasses
3. home   11. dark
4. silk   12. house
5. store   13. candle
6. mouse   14. paper
7. bread   15. eat
8. candy   16. noon

D. Can See Relationships

Page 180   1. day   9. fish
2. book   10. fish
3. birds   11. ear
4. coffee   12. bathroom
5. summer   13. thirteen
6. hospital   14. walk
7. Easter   15. nose
8. plane   16. table

Page 181   1. gas   7. orange, black
2. walk   8. computer
3. hit   9. write
4. sea (water)   10. fish
5. trousers (jeans, pants)   11. cook
6. barns (stables)

Page 182   1. below   11. a long way off
2. near   12. in a low place
3. above   13 end
4. highest point   14. middle
5. first   15. within
6. ahead   16. from high to low
7. in this spot   17 beginning
8. toward the rear   18. stop
9. lowest point   19. halfway
10. back   20. ahead

Page 183   1. beginning   8. ahead of time
2. then   9. at this moment
3. at no time   10. always
4. forever   11. end
5. stop   12. next
6. first   13. tardy
7. before long   14. beside

Page 184   1. cold   8. hot dogs
2. Indian   9. Christmas
3. thermometer   10. fall
4. airplane   11. father
5. tire   12. sentence
6. museum   13. cow
7. seals   14. horse

E. Can Predict Outcomes

Page 185
Any logical answer given by the student is acceptable. Answers will vary depending on the students' experiences.

Page 186
Any logical answer given by the student is acceptable. Answers will vary depending on the students' experiences.

Answer Key

Page 187
Any logical answer given by the student is acceptable. Answers will vary depending on the students' experiences.

Page 188
1. c	4. a
2. b	5. b
3. a	6. b

Page 189
1. b	4. a
2. c	5. b
3. b	6. a

F. Can Follow Printed Directions

Page 190
1. leaves	6. sneaker
2. Rams	7. station
3. bicycle	8. tooth
4. woods	9. Maria
5. desert	10. grilled cheese

Page 191

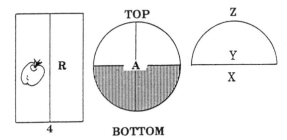

Page 192

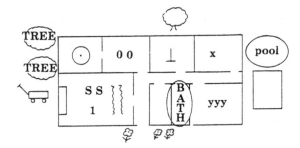

Page 193

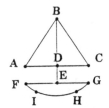

Page 194
1. television set	7. highways
2. spring	8. moonlight, night, bright
3. drugstore	9. tall, high
4. two	10. tale tail
5. (any type of shoe is acceptable)	11. lunch
6. hot	12. silver

G. Can Read for a Definite Purpose

Page 195
1. To obtain an answer to a question
2. To obtain an answer to a question
3. For pleasure
4. To obtain an answer to a question
5. For pleasure
6. For pleasure
7. To obtain an answer to a question
8. For pleasure

Page 196
1. a	7. b
2. b	8. a
3. b	9. b
4. a	10. b
5. b	11. a
6. a	12. b

Page 197
1. b	9. c
2. c	10. b
3. a	11. a
4. b	12. b
5. b	13. c
6. c	14. b
7. a	15. a
8. b	

Page 198
1. b	7. a
2. b	8. b
3. b	9. a
4. c	10. b
5. a	11. c
6. b	12. c

Page 199
1. c	7. c
2. b	8. c
3. a	9. b
4. c	10. c
5. c	11. c
6. a	12. b

Page 200
1. To obtain an answer to a question
2. For pleasure
3. For pleasure
4. For pleasure
5. For pleasure
6. To obtain an answer to a question
7. For pleasure
8. To obtain an answer to a question

Answer Key

Page 201
1. glancing, b
2. read, a
3. searched, a
4. flipped, b
5. writing a report, a
6. laughed, c
7. studied, a
8. read, rushed, a

Page 202
1. c
2. b
3. c
4. d
5. a
6. c
7. c
8. d
9. c
10. b

Page 203
1. c
2. a
3. c
4. d
5. b
6. c
7. c
8. d
9. a
10. c
11. b
12. a

Page 204
1. facts
2. pleasure
3. facts
4. pleasure
5. facts
6. facts
7. pleasure
8. facts
9. pleasure
10. facts
11. facts
12. facts and pleasure

H. Can Classify Items

Page 205
1. c
2. d
3. a
4. h
5. l
6. b
7. g
8. j
9. e
10. k
11. f
12. i

Page 206
1. a
2. b
3. a
4. c
5. b
6. c
7. b
8. b
9. c
10. a

Page 207
1. hat
2. nice
3. angel
4. carrot
5. shirt
6. chimney
7. ring
8. reading
9. uncle
10. grass
11. vine
12. yell
13. once
14. need
15. cover

Page 208
1. runway
2. dog
3. clam
4. flower
5. tennis
6. cry
7. better
8. dark
9. candle
10. butcher
11. family
12. sausage
13. hot
14. jelly
15. ram

Page 209
A. add, sum, multiply, fraction
B. east, south, direction, northwest
C. lasso, cowpuncher, bronco, pen
D. snare, trap, shoot, game

I. Can Use Index

Page 210
1. 85
2. 21-29
3. 88
4. 85
5. 2, 5, 87
6. 70-72
7. 103-107
8. 84-91
9. 66-69
10. 24

Page 211
1. 30
2. 72
3. 38
4. 58
5. 90
6. 22
7. 50
8. 48
9. 105
10. 62
11. 53
12. 10

Page 212
1. 121, 123, 135
2. 21, 36, 92
3. 122, 124
4. 91
5. 150, 154, 160
6. 140
7. 60-65
8. 75, 170, 176
9. 33, 34, 35
10. 60, 61, 62, 63, 64
11. 100, 101
12. 152, 155

Page 213
1. 94-97
2. 185-189
3. 205-206, 218
4. 250
5. 163, 165, 168-170
6. 190, 193, 197
7. 10, 14, 18, 29
8. 9, 12, 19, 21
9. 184, 258, 301
10. 253
11. 258-264
12. 101, 103, 108

Page 214
1. 34, 35, 49
2. 12
3. 29
4. 105
5. 24, 35
6. 39
7. 41
8. 81
9. 14
10. 88, 89, 90
11. 46, 57
12. 1, 2, 3, 55
13. 73
14. 99, 100, 101

J. Can Alphabetize Words by First Two Letters

Page 215
A. 1, 2, 4, 3, 5
B. 5, 3, 1, 4, 2
C. 3, 5, 1, 4, 2
D. 4, 1, 3, 5, 2
E. 2, 5, 3, 4, 1
F. 4, 1, 2, 5, 3
G. 5, 2, 4, 3, 1
H. 4, 5, 2, 1, 3
I. 3, 1, 5, 2, 4
J. 3, 1, 4, 5, 2
K. 4, 1, 3, 5, 2
L. 5, 2, 4, 3, 1

Page 216
1. arctic
2. awake
3. barrel
4. bottom
5. coin
6. cream
7. fact
8. fiction
9. laugh
10. lump
11. match
12. moose
13. paw
14. phone
15. pour
16. school
17. speech
18. squirrel
19. strong
20. syrup

Page 217
1. Vance Bowen
2. Mary Broome
3. Paul Case
4. Jon Clark
5. Phena Fox
6. Wilfred French
7. Blake Gann
8. Mary Gibbs
9. Jack Hartnett
10. Pete Hogan

Answer Key

	11. Judy Jasper	16. Terry Lee
	12. Robert Jones	17. Clara Moss
	13. Sandra Kent	18. Ed Myers
	14. Bobby Knight	19. Sue Wade
	15. Mae Lang	20. Shirley White

Page 218
A. 2, 6, 1, 4, 3, 5   F. 1, 6, 5, 4, 2, 3
B. 1, 3, 5, 2, 4, 6   G. 4, 2, 3, 1, 5, 6
C. 5, 1, 3, 6, 2, 4   H. 5, 2, 4, 6, 1, 3
D. 2, 5, 3, 4, 1, 6   I. 3, 1, 5, 2, 6, 4
E. 2, 5, 4, 6, 1, 3

Page 219
A. 2, 4, 5, 3, 1   G. 4, 1, 3, 5, 2
B. 2, 3, 1, 4, 5   H. 1, 5, 4, 2, 3
C. 3, 5, 2, 1, 4   I. 2, 5, 1, 4, 3
D. 4, 2, 5, 1, 3   J. 2, 1, 3, 4, 5
E. 5, 1, 4, 2, 3   K. 3, 4, 5, 2, 1
F. 3, 2, 5, 1, 4   L. 3, 2, 5, 4, 1

K. Knows Technique of Skimming

Page 220
1. 10:00
2. 8
3. 3
4. 7:00
5. "The Lone Cowboy"
6. "Journey to the Moon"
7. 1 hour
8. 8
9. 4
10. 7:00

Page 221
1. p. 80
2. Business
3. Movies
4. p. 90
5. International Affairs
6. Books
7. Religion
8. National News
9. Newsmakers

Page 222
1. False
2. False
3. True
4. True
5. False
6. True
7. False
8. True

Page 223
1. tunnel or hole
2. an animal with sharp teeth whose teeth continue to grow as their points are worn away by gnawing
3. 16 inches
4. a shrill bark
5. to nap or for safety when danger is nearby
6. True
7. False
8. False
9. False
10. True

Page 224
1. False
2. True
3. False
4. False
5. True
6. True
7. 355-6528
8. Rankin Reds
9. 8:00 PM
10. Bishop Kings

L. Can Determine Source to Obtain Information

Page 225
1. c
2. a
3. c
4. d
5. b
6. f
7. e
8. f
9. a
10. d
11. b
12. e

Page 226
1. b
2. c
3. d
4. e
5. a
6. c
7. d
8. f

Page 227
1. e
2. d
3. g
4. c
5. h
6. k
7. b
8. l
9. a
10. f
11. j
12. i

Page 228
Part I
1. f
2. d
3. e
4. c
5. a
6. b
Part II
1. d
2. f
3. e
4. a
5. c
6. b

Page 229
1. b
2. c
3. a
4. d
5. b
6. a
7. c
8. d
9. c
10. a
11. c
12. b

M. Can Use Maps and Charts

Page 230
1. September
2. February
3. 9
4. March
5. less
6. February
7. October
8. yes

Page 231
1. 8
2. 5
3. ducks
4. donkeys
5. chickens
6. 15
7. number of animals
8. Answer will vary with each child.

Page 232
1. Smith Street
2. 30
3. Shady Avenue
4. Nickel Avenue
5. 8
6. Lincoln Drive
7. Number of houses on each street
8. no

Page 233
4. 114, 118
5. Registration
6. Wading pool
8. North

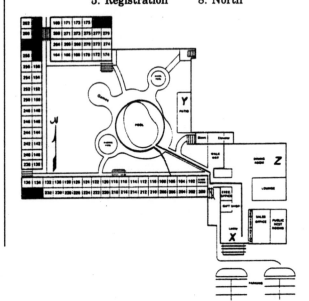

Page 234

1. Blue Street
2. north and south
3. no
4. Green Street and Davis Avenue
5. corner of Brown Street and Jones Avenue
6. west
7. north and south
8. Three
9. east and west
10. Green Street and Smith Avenue

Class Record of Reading Skills
FIRST LEVEL

On the following pages you will find copies of a Class Record of Reading Skills: THIRD LEVEL. This can be used to record the progress of your entire class or an individual child in mastering the specific skills at the Third Level.

The Class Record can help you identify groups of students who need instruction in a particular skill and to assess the relative strengths and levels of individual students. The Class Record can also be used in conferences with administrators, parents and students to discuss reading skills progress.

Name of Teacher: _____

CLASS RECORD OF
READING SKILLS
THIRD LEVEL

Student Names

	I. Vocabulary:	A. Recognizes Dolch 220 Basic Sight Words	B. Word Meaning	1. Comprehends and uses correctly the following words:	Function Words	Forms of Address	Action Words	Direction Words	Metric Words	Color Words	Career Words	Curriculum Words	II. Word Analysis:	A. Refine phonics skills	1. All initial consonant sounds	2. Short and long vowel sounds	3. Changes in words	4. Vowel rules	5. C sound	6. G sound	7. Silent letters in kn, wr, gm	B. Knows skills of	1. Forming plurals	2. Similarities of sound such as x and cks	3. Can read Roman numerals I, V, X	C. Syllabication rules	1. There are usually as many syllables in a word as there are vowels

2. Where there is a single consonant between two vowels, the vowel goes with the first syllable

3. When there is a double consonant, the syllable break is between the two consonants and one is silent

D. Can hyphenate words using syllable rules

E. Understands use of primary accent mark

F. Knows to accent first syllable, unless it is a prefix, otherwise accent second syllable

III. Comprehension

A. Can find main idea in story

B. Can keep events in proper sequence

C. Can draw logical conclusions

D. Is able to see relationships

E. Can predict outcomes

F. Can follow printed directions

G. Can read for a definite purpose

1. for pleasure

2. to obtain answer to question

3. to obtain general idea of content

H. Classify items

I. Use index

J. Alphabetize words by first two letters

K. Knows technique of skimming

L. Can determine what source to obtain information

M. Use maps and charts

IV. Oral and Silent Reading:

A. Oral Reading

1. Reads with expression

2. Comprehends material read aloud

B. Silent Reading

1. Reads silently without finger pointing, lip movements

2. Comprehends material read silently

3. Reads faster silently than orally

C. Listening

1. Comprehends material read aloud by another

2. Can follow directions read aloud